MW00875704

My Father's Final Word?

Jesus, the Word of God, Sword of the Spirit

"… and His name is called
The Word of God. "
Rev 19:13

Johan P Fourie

PRESS

Copyright © 2007 by Johan P Fourie

My Father's Final Word?
by Johan P Fourie

Printed in the United States of America

ISBN 978-1-60266-296-4

All rights reserved solely by the author. The author guarantees all contents are original and do not infringe upon the legal rights of any other person or work. No part of this book may be reproduced in any form without the permission of the author. The views expressed in this book are not necessarily those of the publisher.

Unless otherwise indicated, Bible quotations are taken from the Modern King James Version of the Bible. Copyright © 1962-1998 by Jay P Green, Sr.

www.xulonpress.com

Michelle,

With much love +
blessings!
Be blessed, be free, be
abundantly prosperous in Him!

John & Marie
Soul Safari
July 2007
Africa.

—ɱ—

*" That this little book has fallen into your hands
is an indication that God desires to do
a special work in your heart."*
- *Anonymous* -

Contents

—⚶—

Dedication

—ɱ—

*There is only one possible dedication when
you write about God's Word:*

*All the honour, glory and praises goes to
my Heavenly Father... My Father, my Father...
Abba, I praise You and worship You in the Name
of Your Son Jesus, through the Holy Spirit.*

Preface

—ɯɯ—

The idea to write this book initially dropped into my spirit three years ago. I love and have a hunger for God's Word, and by the grace of God, I receive wonderful revelation knowledge (the Holy Spirit revealing Jesus Christ through Scripture) whilst spending time at His feet. This happens to such an extent that the stream of Holy Spirit revelation sometimes flows at such a rate that I am too slow to write down everything.

Out of the abundance of the heart, the mouth speaks and I love to share this revelation with fellow believers. I have come to the conclusion that the majority of God's children receive very little revelation from the Word itself that really impact and change their lives.

I believe that this saddens God. His will, and also my wish with the writing of this book, is that every believer will taste the richness of God's Word and will experience the depths of His wisdom and revelation... which is Jesus, the indwelling Christ (See my other books *So Who Are You Anyway?* and *There Is Gold On Your Inside!*)

God is not a respecter of person, and with a little bit of light by the grace of God, it is every believer's portion to have a daily revelatory plate of manna at the already prepared feastly table of the LORD.

It is my hope that this book will inspire you and stimulate your hunger for revelation knowledge, or at least challenge some conventional comfort zones in many a life – all to the glory of God alone!

Jesus is the Word of God (Rev 19:13) - that is His new name... He is God's yes and amen (2 Cor 1:20), and not one word of God will return empty or void (Is 55:11). Whilst Jesus is The Word of the Father, we are a word of God, and together as a sentence and as the body, we make up beautiful harmonious sentences for the world to read. He, that is the Volume of the Book, are written on the hearts of people for all the world to read (2 Cor 3:3-8).

Therefore, for those that overcome by the blood of the Lamb and the Word of their testimony (which is Jesus) as stated in Rev 12:11, He will write His new Name upon you, which is the Word of God, which is the Christ within! This will change your thinking of yourself forever - for Jesus is written all over your very being, oozing, flowing from your every pore. If you can believe it in a childlike manner, then you will see the kingdom of God (Luke 17:21).

There is a true story about a Jew that married a Christian lady without really knowing what he was getting himself into... She started evangelising his family and friends.

After a while he was begging her to stop evangelising and telling his friends and family about Jesus, for he was so afraid that he would also loose the already dwindling group of friends all. Surprisingly she agreed, but she had one request. Standing in front of this taller than life husband of hers, and tapping him on the chest with her forefinger, she requested the following: "I will, if you will promise me you will ask your God, the God of your father Abraham ...who this Jesus is!"

He answered yes in order to silence her. Then, a month or two later, he went fishing and whilst casting, his conscience reminded him of his promise... And being an orthodox Jew, he always kept his word.

" Ok God, who is this Jesus anyway?" he asked.

He later testified that the next moment it was if his eyes changed into X-rays and he looked right through his skin into his veins... On every cell, every pore, every bone marrow cell, every blood cell were written Jeshua.. Jeshua.. Jeshua.. Everywhere he looked, right through his whole body, the words Jesus, Jesus, Jesus were written...

Needless to say that he immediately accepted Jesus as his Saviour.

This true story and testimony changed the way I worship for ever - for now I know and feel my every cell shouting out the Name above all Names when I worship my King and my Lord...

It also helped me to grow in my understanding of Scripture reading; Jesus being the "Word of God" and that it is written on the tables of my heart.. (Heb 8) and all over me (Rev 2:13 and 3:17). I am a word within the Word that will not return empty or void to my Father, but was sent forth to accomplish what He wants me to accomplish.

Eat the scroll, the Tree of Life, the Book of Life (Rev/Ezek) Jesus on the inside (Col 1:27), Jesus in every scripture...

Let it be sweet in your mouth; open your mouth wide let Him fill you, let it be bitter in your stomach. Meditate upon it and allow Him to give it to you in your dreams. For He loves you dearly and want to sup and commune with you - bone of His bone and flesh of His flesh (Eph 5 :30-31). He, the Word, wants to become flesh (John 1:1)... on your inside (Col 1:27) - one with Him, in Him (1 John 3:6), one with the

Father (John 17). Believe this with childlike faith and let it permiate your whole being. Let it renew your mind, the mind of Christ (1 Cor 2:16, Rom 12:1-2)

Let Him, let Him, dear child of God, change you from the inside out... As you start to read this book, let the anointing of the Holy Spirit hit you! Let the anointing open the eyes of your understanding...

I pray, proclaim and prophesy this over everyone who reads this little book, from the heart of my Father... Let Him touch you, let Him change you, let Him renew you – Spirit-quickened verse upon Spirit-quickened verse; for the Word is the Sword of the Spirit (Eph 6:17).

Definitions

—ɯ—

Shadow: A representation, symbol or type reflecting
                   Jesus Christ

Typology: A doctrine or theory of types, a doctrine
                   that things in the Christian dispensation
                   are symbolized or pre-figured in the Old
                   Testament, revealing Jesus Christ. We
                   who believe, as His body, should also
                   reveal Him.

Christology: The theological interpretation of the
                   person and work of Jesus Christ

Eyes of   Spiritual eyes as in Eph 1:18, to under-
understanding: stand, interpret things spiritually.

Leaven: A modifying, alleviating agent that
                   mingles and permeates and changes the
                   original substance. In the Bible the leaven
                   (religious rules, regulations and doctrines)
                   of the Scribes and Pharisees threatened to
                   change and modify the pure faith in Jesus
                   Christ. As leaven causes bread and baked
                   goods to rise, religious leaven caused the

religious crowd to become proud and puffed up, and to reject Jesus Christ.

Every believer should search his/her heart for religious leaven which is counterproductive to experiencing the fullness of Jesus Christ.

undignified: State of behaviour without any formal reserve, constraint, thus being spontaneous and acting whole-heartedly. Jesus Christ ultimately died in an totally undignified manner so that we could be saved. Who are we to think that our dignity is more important than to worship Him spontaneously, with all our might, as David did?

quicken: To make alive, to revive, to animate, to enliven. The Holy Spirit make the Word of God come alive and personal to the reader who is receptive to the leading and teaching of the Holy Spirit.

Fire of the Holy Spirit The Holy Spirit ignites a flame, passion and anointing in the heart of the Spirit-filled believer.

Spirit led: To live a life in a Spirit led way, is to be perceptive and obedient to the promptings and leading of the Holy Spirit and to obey Him without considering your own will or wishes. It is a choice to submit your own flesh and will to the authority of the Holy Spirit.

Introduction

—⚏—

"Your Word is a lamp to my feet, and a light to my path."
Ps 119:105

Do you hear God's voice every time you open your Bible? Do you find answers to your questions and solutions to your problems in His Word? Does the Bible come alive and is it a source of direction for your daily life as it was for David, i e a lamp to your feet and a light to your path? (Ps 119:105)

Unfortunately, the majority of believers will have to answer in the negative.

Permit me to share my personal testimony concerning reading the Bible:

When I was 6 years old, I received my first Bible from my Grandfather and Grandmother Le Roux. I also received a children's Bible from Grandfather Fourie. I underlined a few verses in the book Proverbs in my Bible, and when I was in the seventh grade, our English teacher, Mr Niehaus gave us the following verse, which I wrote in the front of my Bible:

Let your light so shine before men... Mat 5:16

I did not enjoy my middle school years and experienced them as limiting. From time to time I effortlessly received revelation knowledge, but wasted it carelessly. Older folks even said too much Bible reading will literally make you mad. I intensely disliked the hypocritical deacon and elder system so prevalent in our conservative churches during those years.

My parents read their Bibles and the Bible had an important place around the family altar, spiritually speaking. On Friday nights when we arrived at my grandparents' farm for a visit, the Bible was fetched and read and prayers of thanksgiving were said for our safe arrival. Nonetheless, I would not say that my parents and my grandparents set an example with specific regard to the importance of daily personal Bible reading, in depth study or beyond that, any revelatory quickening of Jesus in a Christological way. This, in no way takes away from their effort, love and grace as Christians, but God is a God of more! From time to time they read from the Bible and I underlined a few Scripture verses in my first Bible. Years later and long after I had already left home, I sometimes saw my mother and grandmother doing Bible study.

Back then I seldom read the Bible. The one the pastor read from the pulpit, was the nearest I came to a Bible. I also pocketed my great grandfather's heirloom Bible that he used on St Helena, which should have gone to my uncle Koos Le Roux. At that stage it held more importance for my identification with the Boere soldiers and their tradition, than with my love for the Bible itself. Later my parents took this Bible and gave it to its rightful owner. I then inherited the Dutch Family Bible. Years later, in 1996, I started buying my own cheap study Bibles.

After we recommitted our lives to the Lord in Oct 1996, I worked through the whole Bible (the Old Translation Afrikaans version). During this time and at the beginning of my intimate walk with the Lord, I sometimes struggled with the Lord till late at night, occasionally until 03:00. This was especially true of the Old Testament - in particular king David and his doings, the seven sons and grandsons of Saul that were hung while their mothers had to wait on their bodies. This really upset me. I could not understand how God could permit this to happen.

The cross and the baptism with the Holy Spirit brought a turning point, which enlightened the eyes of my understanding so that I could begin to enjoy the wonderful shadow types, and to progressively understand the symbolic meanings of the Spirit driven language and revelation. The more time I spend in the Word, working through and meditating on Scripture from various Bibles in a Spirit filled way, the more God reveals Himself in an awesome manner. It is unimaginable grace, in spite of my repeated falling and standing up again (Prov 24:16). ...until the day breaks and the Morning Star rises in my heart, and the fullness that I already possess, is not contaminated and hindered by my wrong thinking!

Today I feed from the Word every single day and through His grace, it tastes sweet in my mouth... yet sometimes bitter in my stomach. A greater thirst for the sweeter Wine. God's Holy Spirit gives life to my Bible reading. Like a child, I cannot wait and remain full of anticipation to see and experience the new revelation God's gift of the Word and wonders will offer.

My wife, Marié's testimony:

"I gave my heart to the Lord as a young child. I grew up with the Bible. My father regularly read Bible and held devotions for our family. Every night, before going to bed, I read the Bible and prayed. On the occasion that I forgot and had already switched off my light, I felt so guilty that I would get up again to read and pray.

Throughout the difficult times in my life, my faith in Jesus Christ and the Bible were my anchors that kept me going. But at times, I still felt there had to be more – especially when I listened to Spirit-filled people bringing a message of hope and salvation.

After I recommited my life to the Lord 10 years ago, and started attending a Spirit-filled and led congregation where the Holy Spirit was allowed to flow freely, I then realised what it was that I had missed.

I took the promise of the Holy Spirit to heart and asked Spirit-filled believers to lay hands upon me and to pray for the baptism of the Holy Spirit.

After that, a brand new wonder (Spirit) world of the Word opened up to me. The Lord started speaking to me personally and I received answers to my questions and promises of things to come concerning certain problem areas in my life. The Bible that I had read since my childhood, and some parts already well-known to me, were quickened and given life through the Holy Spirit teaching me. I started looking at verses, words, and meanings with the new, eager and uncontaminated eyes of a child.

I started living the Word and started writing in my Bible. My early morning time spent at Abba's feet became very precious – today I still do not want to miss it. During this time I receive awesome revelations – revelations, I now realize, were always my portion as well as that of every believer – if we will just believe it and receive it! I started to write down these revelations in journals. Now, even after 10 years, whenever I read some of my first revelations, I again realize how wonderful God is and in what an awesome way He uses His Spirit to lead us and teach us - if only we are available and willing!

The Lord's mercies are new every morning! It will never change. Our Father knows in detail what you and I need every day. Open wide your heart and your mouth (Psalm 81:10), let the King of Glory come in and fill you to overflowing with His glorious living Bread. If you have tasted it once, you will not be able to live without it!

If I may ask you once more: Do you hear God's voice every time you open your Bible? Do you receive answers to your questions, solutions to your problems, and practical advice for everyday living from the Word?

In this book you will learn how to change your no or faltering yes to a heartfelt yes, and how to hear God's voice every time you open your Bible. It is His will for <u>you</u>! Today can be the beginning of a new and exciting faith walk that will exceed everything you can think or pray! (Eph 3:20)

A lot has been written on the subject of Bible reading, and there are also numerous programmes for reading through the Bible in one year. However, to my knowledge, very little has been written from the perspective of the Holy Spirit as teaching and revealing the depths of God, as well as the fact that the Bible should be spiritually discerned because God is Spirit, and only the Spirit of God knows His depths and can reveal Him.

I want to venture out and say that the other Bible study tecniques encompass flesh and soul level, but do not lead to a deeper relationship, transformation and conformation to the full stature of Jesus Christ (Ezek 3:7-8). We should earnestly ask ourselves if our Bible reading leads to Jesus' life springing up inside ourselves and also in the lives of other people. Or does it lead to dead religion, intellectual knowledge, a set of morality rules and arguments?

Holy Spirit baptism, through the laying on of hands or through your own heartfelt seeking, will open up a new Spirit world and a deeper and richer relationship - guaranteed (Luke 11:13).

Chapter 1

How Do You Read the Bible?

—ɱ—

Is God's Word precious to you? Centuries ago, men because of their love for and faith in the Bible as the irrefutable Word of God, made sacrifices. John Wycliff, that translated the Bible into English, and William Tyndale who paid with his life so that the Bible could be put into the hands of the man on the street, endured persecution and suffering.

In the Western world, the Word of God is freely available – to such an extent that people usually have more than one Bible – Bibles that are collecting dust and are seldom, if ever used.

In other countries and parts of the world, because Christians are persecuted for their faith, their Bibles become their most precious possession – and something for which they are willing to die. Some of them do not even possess a Bible, or it is taken away from them.

Brother Yun, one of China's house church leaders, endured a lot of persecution for his faith, and testifies about this in his book "The Heavenly Man":

"I had no Bible with me, so I meditated on God's Word from memory... I shouted out Bible verses at the top of my voice, clinging to God's promises.... [1]

"I had written Scriptures from the Gospel of John and 1 Peter on a long piece of toilet paper. I fashioned it into a belt of truth, fastening the Word of God around my waist." [2]

All of this took place while he was in prison – beaten and nearly kicked to death because of his faith.

How often do we read the Bible?
According to a poll[3] of 1000 adults randomly selected in America in 1990, and 1559 adults in 1986, the following transpired:

Percentage	1990	1986	1982	1978	
1990 Statistics	%	%	%	%	
Daily or more often	17	11	15	12	
Weekly or more often	23	22	18	18	
Once a month or more often	13	14	12	11	
Less than once a month	25	26	25	28	
Rarely or never	20	22	24	24	
Can't say	2	5	6	7	
1986 Statistics	Every day	1 x week	1 x month	Less than 1 x month	Never
Nationwide	11	22	14	26	22
Men	8	18	12	30	27
Women	15	25	16	22	17
Whites	11	21	14	26	23
Blacks	17	31	12	21	15
Protestants	18	27	15	23	12
Catholics	4	16	13	32	31
Evangelicals	29	37	15	15	4
Non-evangelicals	4	15	13	31	30

How about you?

Do you regularly read, study, and meditate the Bible on your own? Or are you part of the majority of people who rarely if ever open and read the Bible for themselves?

Answer the following questions in order to evaulate your own habits?

How often do you read the Bible? *(Circle one)*

Never
Once a month
Once a week
2-3 times week
Every day
2 or more times a day

When you read, how much time do you spend reading the Bible?

5 min or less   15 min   30 min   45 min   1 hour or more

People give the following reasons for not reading the Bible. Check the ones that also apply to you.

.... The Bible is not relevant to my life.

.... The Bible is difficult to understand.

.... I used to read the Bible, and it made me feel good. But after a while, it did not seem to have the same impact.

.... I feel guilty when I read the Bible.

.... The Bible is out-of date. It contains interesting stories but these are not applicable to everyday life.

.... I rely on my pastor/cell leader to explain the Bible to me. They will teach me if there is something I need to know.

.... I doubt the credibility of the Bible.

.... I don't have time. I am too busy.

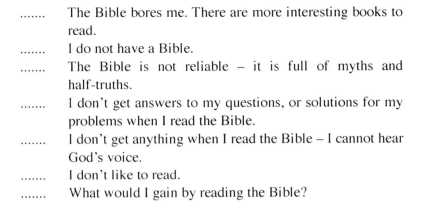

.... The Bible bores me. There are more interesting books to read.

.... I do not have a Bible.

.... The Bible is not reliable – it is full of myths and half-truths.

.... I don't get answers to my questions, or solutions for my problems when I read the Bible.

.... I don't get anything when I read the Bible – I cannot hear God's voice.

.... I don't like to read.

.... What would I gain by reading the Bible?

***His mercies never fail. They are new every morning;
great is Your faithfulness.
Lam 3:22-23***

Historically speaking, the Bible (as letters and scrolls and sometimes only Jesus and the Holy Spirit in oral form revealed the Christ within) was read in a Christological and Spirit-driven way until 300 AD – and less frequently in recent times. Believers and church fathers had a personal and inti-mate relationship with the Holy Spirit (Eph 3:14-16, Rom 11, Jer 33:3) Some congregations in Galatia didn't even have access to Christian or Hebrew holy writings at all, but memo-rized portions about the indwelling Christ as preached for the first time by Paul and Barnabas. What a privilege to have the full inspired Word and to enjoy it to our hearts' content!

When the church was institutionalized, the Bible then became a set of morality rules, thus losing its Spirit-driven interpretation that was so prevalent during the first three centuries. During this period of the Dark Middle Age, the Latin Bible was not available to the man in the street, but only to church fathers which interpreted it in a allegoric, moral and anagogical manner, thus introducing mystical elements applicable to the soul level.

It rendered the theology of Paul as very mystical for the common man, perverted the words of the apostle and lead to the translation of the Bible into English by John Wycliffe and John Hus in the 14th century, thereby making it available to all. [4]

As a backlash to the mystical elements of interpretation, John Colet let the Scriptures speak to directly to the people in the pew, but only in the literal and practical sense – thus more intellectual in nature. William Tyndale and Martin Luther in the 16th century translated the Bible in a practical manner to be read and taken at face value, which gave rise to the First and glorious Reformation (saved through faith by grace) and again ventured into a deeper level of interpretation. But in a sense they never moved into the fullness and multidimensional Spirit-driven revelation quoted in Eph 6:17, that God had intended for His children.

I believe this will lead to the Second and last Reformation leading the children of God into fullness, Col 2:9-10, and foursquare perfection and revelation, reading and interpreting His Word not in a literal, intellectual or mystical manner, but in a Spirit-driven way, thereby comparing spiritual things with spiritual (1 Cor 2:14). Approximately 500 years back satan tried to stop the translation of the Bible. When that failed, he is now trying to prevent the anointed empowerment of the body of Christ, which is the second part of Eph 6:17 Spirit-driven Word.

Before you want to learn how to read the Bible, you should ask yourself the following question:

Why do I want to read the Bible?

For the Christian the reason should always be to grow spiritually in your walk with God and to deepen your relationship with Him. Jesus Christ should always be the focus, and not your own intellectual knowledge.

It's all about the power of transformation, and acquiring Godly wisdom and knowledge through God's Word and the application of it in your life. It is not about getting more human intellectual knowledge. (Eph 5:26, 2 Pet 3:18, 1 Pet 4:10-11, Hos 4:6, Rom 12:1-2)

James Rutz says the following in his book **Megashift**:

> *"The average person's mind is a randomly acquired patchwork of contradictory slogans, clichés, catch-phrases, and myths, all of which work together at Pentium-chip speed along logic lines that Rube Goldberg could never have dreamed of. You cannot become a mature Christian disciple unless your mind is transformed, and **much of that transformation will come as you study Scripture and let the Holy Spirit teach you**. Read, mark, and reflect on the Word – then act on it. You aren't just trying to learn the Bible, but to know God **through** the Bible – and become like Him."* [5]

Eugene Peterson, who compiled "The Message", says the following:

> *"God works patiently and deeply, but often in hidden ways... The Bible does not give us a predict-able cause-effect world in which we can plan our careers and secure our futures. It is not a dream world in which everything works out according to our adolescent expectations... For most of us it takes years and years and years to exchange our dream world for this real world of grace and mercy, sacrifice and love, freedom and joy—the God-saved world.*
>
> *Yet another surprise is that the Bible does not flatter us... The reality that comes into focus as we read the Bible has to do with what God is doing in a saving love that includes us and everything we do.*

This is quite different from what our sin-stunted and culture-cluttered minds imagined.

God doesn't force any of this on us: God's word is personal address, inviting, commanding, challenging, rebuking, judging, comforting, directing—but not forcing. Not coercing. We are given space and freedom to answer, to enter the conversation. For more than anything else the Bible invites our participation in the work and language of God.

As we read, we find that there is a connection between the Word Read and the Word Lived. Everything in this Book is livable. Many of us find that the most important question we ask as we read is not "What does it mean?" but "How can I live it?" So we read personally, not impersonally. We read in order to live our true selves, not just get information that we can use to raise our standard of living. Bible reading is a means of listening to and obeying God, not gathering religious data by which we can be our own gods.

You are going to hear stories in this Book that will take you out of your preoccupation with yourself and into the spacious freedom in which God is working the world's salvation. You are going to come across words and sentences that stab you awake to a beauty and hope that will connect you with your real life.

Be sure to answer."[6]

Andrew Murray, viewed Bible reading and quiet time with God as following:

"As we listen, meditate, and pray, as we surrender ourselves and accept in faith the whole Jesus as He offers Himself to us in it—the Holy Spirit will make the Word to spirit and life. This word of Jesus, too,

will become to us the power of God unto salvation, and through it will come the faith that grasps the long desired blessing...

It takes time to grow into Jesus the Vine: do not expect to abide in Him unless you will give Him that time. It is not enough to read God's Word...and when we think we have hold of the thoughts and have asked God for His blessing, to go out in the hope that the blessing will abide. No, it requires day-by-day time with Jesus and with God. We all know the need of time for our meals each day...

If we are to live through Jesus, we must feed on Him (John 6:57); we must thoroughly take in that heavenly food the Father has given us in His Word. Therefore, my brother and sister who wants to learn to abide in Jesus, take time each day, before you read, while you read, and after you read, to put your-self into living contact with the living Jesus, to yield yourself distinctly and consciously to His blessed influence, so will you give Him the opportunity of taking hold of you, of drawing you up and keeping you safe in His almighty life."[7]

The well-known author of the Jabez Prayer, and teacher Bruce Wilkenson made the following statement:

"Even though Christians truly find the Lord when they are born again, they certainly have not "found" all of Him. But because this truth isn't widely understood, many Christians don't realize the need to continue seeking God. They stop rising early in order to seek Him through His Word and prayer. Remember, revival is relationship. So take some time to evaluate your present relationship with God, and the extent to which you are seeking Him. If deep down

you want revival, then that relationship must be revitalized, either by taking away the negative (sin) or adding to the positive (fellowship with Him). Have you sought Him today?

When we need wisdom, God is eager to provide it. All we have to do is ask. Only one condition applies: "But let him ask in faith, with no doubting, for he who doubts is like a wave of the sea driven and tossed by the wind" (James 1:6)

This concept of doubt, which means "of two minds" in the Bible, is of critical importance. It signifies a more profound spiritual failure than our own modern ideas about doubt. Its precise opposite is the "whole-hearted" faith that is required of us. In essence, it is an attitude about God. It means we approach Him with a fundamental trust in His wisdom and faithfulness. The total mind must seek His wisdom and have full faith in His promises."[8]

Remember that everything that is truly worth it, comes with a price. In this instance, only your time is required – spend time at the feet of King Jesus and let the Holy Spirit lead and teach you, in order to glorify God more and more.

Some of the things you read in this book are repeated often, and may appear difficult to hear and digest. Please bear in mind that in order for seed to fall on fertile soil (of your heart and mind), the soil should be well prepared by approaching matters from different angles. Paul made the following statement in 1 Cor 3:6:

**"I have planted, Apollos watered,
but God gave the increase."**

May you experience it firsthand while reading this book.

Chapter 2

The Approach

—ᴡᴡ—

The insight one has in one single moment, could mean
just as much as the experience of a lifetime.
Oliver Wendell Holmes

The believer's approach to reading the Bible will differ from that of a non-believer.

The believer should read the Bible in a Spirit driven manner, and should rely on the Holy Spirit to guide and teach them, and for revelation.

The non-believer will read driven by his or her intellect and will seek God by searching the Scriptures (John 5:39-44). To them it is more of an obligation or intellectual exercise to seek God through searching the Scriptures.

Matthew Henry explains the searching of Scriptures as follows:

> *The Jews considered that eternal life was revealed to them in their Scriptures, and that they had it, because they had the word of God in their hands. Jesus urged them to search those Scriptures with more diligence and attention. "Ye do search the*

Scriptures," and ye do well to do so. They did indeed search the Scriptures, but it was with a view to their own glory.

It is possible for men to be very studious in the letter of the Scriptures, yet to be strangers to its power. Or, "Search the Scriptures," and so it was spoken to them in the nature of an appeal. Ye profess to receive and believe the Scripture, let that be the judge. It is spoken to us as advising or commanding all Christians to search the Scriptures. Not only read them, and hear them, but search them: which denotes diligence in examining and studying them. We must search the Scriptures for heaven as our great end; for in them ye think ye have eternal life.

We must search the Scriptures for Christ, as the new and living Way, that leads to this end. To this testimony Christ adds reproofs of their unbelief and wickedness, their neglect of him and his doctrine. Also he reproves their want of the love of God. But there is life with Jesus Christ for poor souls. Many make a great profession of religion, yet show they don't want the love of God, by their neglect of Christ and contempt of his commandments.

It is the love of God in us, the love that is a living, active principle in the heart, which God will accept. They slighted and undervalued Christ, because they admired and overvalued themselves. How can those believe, who make the praise and applause of men their idol! When Christ and his followers are men wondered at, how can those believe, the utmost of whose ambition is to make a fair show in the flesh!"[9]

Unfortunately a large percentage of Christians never make the transition from pure intellectual communion with the Word of God to Spirit driven revelation (2 Cor 3, 1 Cor

2). It is only when the stream of living Holy Spirit-driven revelation start to flow, that the Word of God will come alive for you, and you will never become satiated. Then, and only then, the Word will become your daily Bread that will fill and lead you every day, without which you cannot live.

Howard Hendricks made the following statement, based on statistics:

> ***"In effect, when it comes to scripture, the
> normal person is functionally illiterate six
> out of seven days a week...
> Dusty Bibles lead to dirty lives.
> In fact you are either in the Word and
> the Word is conforming you to the image
> of Christ, or you are in the world and the
> world is squeezing you into its mould."*[10]**

Only 10 % of all Americans read the Bible every day. 15% of women and only 8% of men read their Bibles every day.

Pray and ask God to reveal Himself to you through His Word – It is also Paul's prayer for every believer in Eph 1:17-18:

> *"that the God of our Lord Jesus Christ, the Father of glory,
> may give to you the spirit of wisdom
> and revelation in the knowledge of Him,
> the eyes of your understanding being enlightened,
> that you may know what is the hope of His calling,
> and what is the riches of the glory
> of His inheritance in the saints,"*

To read and comprehend the depths and riches of the Bible, will probably prove more difficult to both the non-believer and the believer who reads the Bible without being baptised with the Holy Spirit. This is because God, who is Spirit, reveals a Holy Spirit driven message about Himself to the world, through His Son, Jesus Christ (Heb 11:1).

But, that being said, theologians also state that liguistically and in terms of comprehension, the Bible is written on a Grade 6 level ... probably one of the reasons the Jewish "Bar mitzvah" takes place at the age of 13 years. The children's song declares aptly:

Read your Bible, pray every day...

Without the Spirit (2 Cor 3) the Word of God will not transform you to conform to the full stature of Christ (Eph 4:13). You have to know the Writer before you can understand what He has written (Jer 33:3 and Rom 11:33 speaks of the depths of God's riches, wisdom and knowledge, and Rom 12:1-2 speaks of His perfect will).

At least the following guideline should apply to all of us when reading the Bible:

"The Bible is designed to be read as living literature."
E S Bates

The Word of God is compared to the following shadow types:

- The Name of all names Jesus Christ, the Word of God (Rev 19:13).
- A sword (Ezek 23:6, Eph 6:13 and Heb 4:12)
- A mirror (2 Cor 3:18)
- A record of the words of the Father, Jesus, the Son and the Holy Spirit (Gen 1, John 1, Heb 1)
- A lamp unto your feet and a light unto your path (Ps 119)
- A washing by the water (Eph 5:26)

- Offense (Matt 15:12)
- Becoming flesh (John 1)
- Streams of living water (Rev 22)
- And others.

The Word of God is also God-breathed, and is profitable for doctrine, for reproof, for correction, for instruction in righteousness (2 Tim 3:16).

Read Ezek 34, 1 John 2:27, Heb 8:10 and see what the Word of God teaches you concerning reading and understanding the Bible.

Matthew Henry summarises it:

"Those who would learn the things of God, and be assured of them, must know the Holy Scriptures, for they are the Divine revelation. The age of children is the age to learn; and those who would get true learning, must get it out of the Scriptures. They must not lie by us neglected, seldom or never looked into. The Bible is a sure guide to eternal life. The prophets and apostles did not speak from themselves, but delivered what they received of God, 2 Pet 1:21. It is profitable for all purposes of the Christian life. It is of use to all, for all need to be taught, corrected, and reproved. There is something in the Scriptures suitable for every case. Oh that we may love our Bibles more, and keep closer to them! Then shall we find benefit, and at last gain the happiness therein promised by faith in our Lord Jesus Christ, who is the main subject of both Testaments. We best oppose error by promoting a solid knowledge of the word of truth; and the greatest kindness we can do to children, is to make them early to know the Bible."[11]

Prophets are Word eaters and Word speakers. Jesus asks Peter in John 21:15-17:

"Do you love me?"

When he aswered in the affirmative, Jesus gave him the following command:

"Feed My lambs." and later *"Feed My sheep."*

How do we feed God's people? By giving them the Word of God – not on the intellectual level, but revealed by the Holy Spirit. That means you need the revealed Word of God in yourself, before you can feed others. If not, you cannot be obedient to the command Jesus gave to Peter and to all of us.

Peter 4:10-11 says that when we speak, our words should be like God's words, which can only be the case if God's written Word, the Bible, lives in your heart and spirit. For out of the abundance of the heart, the mouth speaks.

Chapter 3

Jesus the Focus

—~~—

If you see Jesus in everything, you will also see blessings in everything.

What does it mean to read the Bible Christologically? It simply yet profoundly means to see Jesus in all Scripture and to make Him your central focus.

When you see Jesus in all Scripture you read, you will also see the blessing in everything, and the Word will come alive, because Jesus Christ is the Word:

" In the beginning was the Word,
and the Word was with God,
and the Word was God.
He was in the beginning with God.
John 1:1-2

"The light of reason, as well as the life of sense, are derived from him, and depend upon him. This eternal Word, this true Light shines, but the darkness comprehends it not. Let us pray without ceasing, that our eyes may be opened to behold this Light, that we

may walk in it; and thus be made wise unto salvation, by faith in Jesus Chris)."[12]

When looking at the word "Christological", the following can be said:

The word can be broken up in two parts:

Christ which means "Anointed" = Oil of the Holy Spirit, which leads to revelation knowledge.

Logic: The only logical way to read the Bible is with the aid and guidance of the Holy Spirit flowing through you. It also means to be Word wise, ie to live in the wisdom of God, which is Jesus Christ. (Gen 1, John 1, Heb 1, Rev 19:13.)

Logos: The only way you can receive the full revelation is with the baptism and anointing of the Holy Spirit flowing through you. Then and only then, the Logos Word (written Word) can become the Rhema (revelation) Word.

Jesus Christ is the Word of God (Rev 19:13). Jesus is the golden or scarlet thread running through the Bible – right from the first chapter in Genesis to the last one in Revelation. Therefore everything in the Word should be brought back to Jesus Christ, and many concepts in the Old and New Testament are shadow types and types that points to Jesus, e.g. kid of goats (sin offering), the ark's mercy seat, veil, the blood on the door posts, the Lamb that was slain, etc.

The spiritual symbolism (see Chapter 8) will open up a new and exciting Spirit world to you, that will be your entry into understanding the depths of God's love for you, His precious child, and the wonder of His grace and power. Only when the logos becomes rhema through the Holy Spirit, the Word comes alive and Jesus will start to flow through you in streams of living water. You will discover that the Word of God is living and powerful, that it never returns to Him void, but always accomplishes that for which He sent it.

The following true story bears testimony to this promise in Is 55:11:

In the summer of 1965, the entire family had gathered for a family reunion in Plant City, Florida. At 2:00 A.M., my grandmother woke everyone and started issuing orders to get empty Coke bottles, corks and blank paper ready.

I've received a message from God," she said. "People must hear His Word.'"

She started writing verses on the paper, while all of the grandchildren bottled and corked the passages. That morning, everyone drove to Cocoa Beach and deposited more than two hundred bottles into the surf.

Over the years, people wrote, called and visited my grandmother, always thanking her for the scripture. She died in November 1974. In December of 1974, <u>the last letter arrived and it stated</u>:

Dear Mrs. Cause,

I'm writing this letter to you by candlelight. We no longer have electricity on the farm. My husband was killed in the fall when the tractor overturned on him. He left eleven children and myself behind. They're all under the age of fourteen. The bank is foreclosing; there's one loaf of bread left; there's snow on the ground; Christmas is two weeks away. I prayed to the Lord to forgive me, before I went to the river to drown myself. It's been frozen over for weeks now, so I didn't think it would take long. I had to break the ice, and as I did, a Coke bottle floated up. I opened it, and with tears and trembling hands, I read about hope, Ecclesiastes 9:4:

*"But for him who is joined to all the
living there is hope for a living dog
is better than a dead lion."*

*You went on to reference other Scriptures:
Hebrew 7:19, 6:18, John 3:3.*

*I came home and read my Bible, and now
I'm thanking God for the message. We're
going to make it now. Please pray for us, but
know we're all right.*

May God bless you and yours.

A farm in Ohio
Chrystle White[13]

A Word seed, sown in faith and obedience, a mustard seed that lay in the "soil" for 9 years, before it became a mighty tree of Hope!

The Bible can be read at three levels:

- <u>Carnal</u>: (Outer Court)

    This entails reading and interpreting the Bible on a purely intellectual level by using the mental faculties only. Most believers read the Bible in such a manner, and then use other books, commentaries and daily devotional books during their time spent at God's feet.

    It is not wrong to use these aids and books, but it should never be used during your quiet time. The reason for this statement is that the lesson and revelation that God gave the person writing the message, is not necessarily the lesson and revelation He wants to give to you.

42

During your quiet time your primary aim should always be firsthand communication with your Heavenly Father, Abba. Hereby your personal and very unique intimate relationship with Him will be built – without another person's subjective opinion and revelations intruding.

Often, the daily devotion or commentary blesses you at that moment, but a day or two later you don't even remember what you read. It therefore has only momentary worth, but does not transform you or change your life. That is because you did not receive the revelation from the Holy Spirit, and therefore He could not quicken it and write it on the table of your heart, never to be forgotten!

- Soul level: (Inner Court)

    This entails a deeper form of reading and by allowing the water of the Word to literally "brain wash" your mind from wrong thinking. It changes your life and relationships in a practical manner, but is still self-centered and often leads to own effort and dead works, and only temporary change. This is a deeper level of reading the Bible, the milk that Paul speaks of in 1 Cor 3:2, but still falls short of the richness and abundance of revelation with which the Lord wants to feed and bless us from His word.

- Spiritual level: (Holy of Holies)

    The main aim when reading the Bible is progressive Spirit-driven revelation whereby the Holy Spirit quickens a verse or portion of Scripture and makes it personally applicable, to such an extent that you will never forget it. It leads to a Spirit-filled life that will change you and everyone you encounter.

Once you have experienced this level of Bible reading, you will never again be satisfied with less than the best. It is the solid food spoken about in Heb 5:14, that will nourish you and let you grow and be transformed from one level of glory to the full glory of Jesus Christ (2 Cor 3:18), until the full stature of Jesus Christ will be visible for all to see (Gal 4:19)

This is only possible when you have been baptized with the Holy Spirit, and He has exploded the Word to such an extent that you receive your Spirit tongue and new name (identity in Christ) progressively every day through Spirit-driven Word revelation.

Christology is powerfully illustrated in the Word in Hebrews 9 where the Ark of the Covenant and the tabernacle serve as shadow types of Jesus, and where Father invites you to enter boldly.

Chapter 4

Guidelines

—ᴜᴜ—

Enjoy a fresh portion of the living Bread every morning and evening.

1. Get fresh manna every day (Ex 16:21). Begin and end your day with a piece of fresh bread out of God's word by reading your Bible every morning and every evening before you fall asleep. God wants to speak to you every day, and knows much better than you what you need each day.

2. Every day lay down all your intellectual knowledge about God and His word before Him. Ask God to teach you, and to give you Spirit-driven revelation for that day (fresh bread, fresh fountain water, fresh manna) in Jesus' Name, Him being the Bread of Life (John 6:35) and the Word of God (Rev 19:13).

3. Know and measure what you read and be sure to jot it down.
    Example:
    Morning: 15 minutes John 1
    Revelation you received from the above reading?

... The Word (Jesus) became flesh, etc...

In other words jot down the specific revelation, which God gave you, as well as the specific words and verses that spoke to you. It is important to make a note of the specific verse as well as the revelation – more often than not it will later serve as a powerful confirmation of the voice of God and His working in your life. And don't think you will remember it – more than anything the enemy wants to steal every piece of revelation, blessing and abundance from God's heart:

"The thief cometh not, but that he may steal, and
kill,
and destroy: I came that they may have life,
and may have it abundantly."
John 10:10

When you write down the revelation, you will remember much better, and it's much easier to share the revelation with somebody else (see included notes on Hearing God's Voice) Often, the revelation only starts to flow the moment you pick up your pen and start writing! All your sermons and messages will be effortless and for free, flowing forth from your heart, received in the Throne Room of your Father.

Please don't be lazy – the only price you will pay is your time, and your Bibles and journals become a legacy for your children, as well as a daily message for other people crossing your path. Through this the Holy Spirit can speak to others and through this you can have fellowship with other believers. Write in your diary, or another note book and record the revelation you have received in a more specific and detailed manner, over and above what you have highlighted and written down in your

Bible. The Lord very often in His Word commands His prophets to write down what He reveals to them:

> *Now go, write it before them on a tablet,*
> *and inscribe it in a book that it may be*
> *for the time to come for ever and ever.*
> *Isa 30:8*

> *Thus speaketh Jehovah, the God of Israel,*
> *saying, Write thee all the words that*
> *I have spoken unto thee in a book.*
> *Jer 30:2*

> *And Jehovah answered me, and said,*
> *Write the vision, and make it plain upon tablets,*
> *that he may run that readeth it.*
> *Hab 2:2*

And remember the most powerful way to learn is by example. If you want your children and grandchildren to love God's Word, and to receive revelation from it, live according to it, they must see this in your life and your example. For this very reason share your revelation with them when the Holy Spirit leads you to do it.

4. "Attitude in asking the right type of questions", prayerfully, humbly, but also with big boldness to seek God in the throne room (Heb 10):

> *" When the learner is ready,*
> *the teacher will appear!"*

When you as believer becomes available and open, the Holy Spirit will come and teach you and guide you and reveal Jesus to you. And in addition you create a legacy for your children's children – a valuable legacy of the heart. The children of some Godly men and women fought for their old well-used Bibles, which they worked through at least once a year with highlighters, pens etc.

5. Approach the Bible or a book or a verse in the Bible, as Heb 4:12, as you would anything in life that is worth the time and effort to look at with attention. Read it more than once, so that the depths of God as described in Rom 11:33 can be revealed to you. Come to God's Word with great expectation, and be obedient to the revelation you receive, in whatever form. My wife, Marié testifies:

> *One day while I was reading and meditating on James 5:10-12 in the Word of God in my quiet time spent at His feet, a thought dropped into my heart to write a poem concerning the revelation I had just received. As I love words and poems, I was obedient immediately and started to write down as the words started to flow. Afterwards when I read what I had written, I was amazed at the creative flow of the Spirit through me:*

> *3 June 2003 : James 5:10-12*
> *The prophets of old*
> *In James we are told*
> *Persevered and had much patience*
> *In prophesying and speaking to the nations.*
> *Job, in his life also suffered much*
> *But was doubly blessed by God's touch.*
> *The Lord is full of mercy and grace*
> *To every man child He turns His face*
> *To bless him and to keep him safe*
> *If only he will walk in faith.*
> *So don't ever swear by heaven or earth*

But let truth and integrity be your girth
Let your yes be yes and your no no
And let God's living streams of water flow
Speak words of truth and words of life
Without any envy, without any strife.
Let your hands do the acts of God's hand
As in His power and love we stand!

It blessed me and I could share this with fellow believers. After that day of being obedient to the prompting of the Holy Spirit, it happens fairly regularly that God reveals His word to me, in poetic form.

<u>*A portion of a poem written on 9 June 2003*</u>
<u>*James 5;15-20*</u>

So let us be fearless and let us be bold
And do mighty miracles and wonders untold
Because it is Christ who lives in me
Who through the Holy Spirit let me see
What I can accomplish and do in His Name
Without any pride and without any claim.
I come to Your throne of mercy and grace
To gaze upon Your kind and loving face
To be in Your presence and be filled
That Your love, power and mercy
may be instilled.
Then I can go out and say "I can"
And with boldness and faith
pray for every man
Who so desperately needs Your loving touch
For the prayer of the righteous
availeth much!!

God is a creative God and He made us in His image. Release the creative force and anointing of the Holy Spirit, and be obedient to whatever He lays on your heart. Whether it is writing a poem or a story, drawing an image, composing a song, making an object of art, be obedient. He will use the unique creative talents He has deposited in you, to write the revelation He has for you on the tables of your heart, and to share and bless others with it. If you keep Him in the centre, your eyes focussed on Him the author and finisher of our faith.

> ### *Come to God's Word with great expectation.*
> ### *E S Jones*

6. The Word must explain the Word. Scripture must explain Scripture. An awesome revelation would mostly come out of one verse or one little word, but the Holy Spirit will often build something like a puzzle into your Spirit in order to reveal the fullness (Col 2:9-10) of Jesus to you and in you through the Holy Scripture. This causes you to start believing what you have received at your salvation like a little child (with a brain like a sponge, slurping and drinking it like the trunk of an elephant). Then you can that start believing, experiencing and living it.

    We are His body right here on earth, aren't we? Therefore the mind of Christ has already been vested in you.. which happens in a momentary flash the moment you say yes to Jesus. The secret is to let His fullness which has already been deposited in you, flow freely ..release that out of you...boldly and freely. This can only happen if you know how much God loves you, and that perfect love drives out the fear (1 John 4:18)

7. Without the Holy Spirit, the Word stays dim as 1 Cor 13 says. However, Paul says in 2 Cor 3:18 that he has

matured into a man, by looking into a mirror and being changed from one degree of glory to the glory of Christ in us (our salvation, Col 1:27, 1 Cor 1:30, 2 Cor 13:5) to being born again into the full stature of Christ, in order (spiritually speaking) to look more and more like Jesus to a lost world (Eph 4:13; Col 2:9-10). Start to fully depend on the Holy Spirit - it is only by His inspiration that the Bible was written, isn't it?

8. Watch out that your intellectual knowledge of the Word, does not become your identity, and that it makes you feel successful or content with what you know and not who you know. Our intellect is only needed and granted to draw us nearer to God by our growing in knowledge and grace of our Lord Jesus Christ (2 Pet 3:18). Our only true identity that has to grow or be released through the washing of the water by the Word (Eph 5:26), is our identity in Christ, the new man in Christ :

"Wherefore if any man is in Christ, he is a new creature:
the old things are passed away;
behold, they are become new."
2 Cor 5:17

9. Rely 100% on the ability of the Holy Spirit to lead you, teach you and reveal the scriptures to you. He wrote them (and not your pastor or a theology professor... no pun intended on all the Spirit filled professors out there), and thus He reveals Jesus more and more through the Holy Scriptures to you (100%). He is powerful and mighty enough as part of the Trinity and the fullness of the Godhead, isn't He?

The Holy Spirit must and is hands down a better teacher than any doctrinal theologian.... At the most, doctrine should serve as a basis for, but not a relationship in itself with a living God... and the Holy Spirit Himself is also willing and able to reveal sound doctrine to you, if you truly come to the feastly table of the Word with a humble heart, not so much to change others but to be changed yourself.

Don't, please don't rely on your own insight or theological books as a point of departure. This will only serve as additional knowledge to your unique path and application of your life by God, which differs from the particular road map of the life of myself, Paul, Peter, Billy Graham, Solly Osrovech, Benny Hinn, TD Jakes, Kelley Varner, Kobus van Rensburg, Joyce Meyer, or the Hunchback of Notre Dame, Joan of Arc or the murderer on the cross.

God wants to speak to you personally and teach you personally (see included notes on Hearing God's voice). If you grab hold of a book or the secondary teachings of somebody elses revelation, you will in all probability miss what God wants to teach you. You will then also miss how He wants to reach people through you by using His word on a personal basis in your life. It is supposed to be a relationship. Keep in mind that God will not give you all the revelation. His workings through His body and fellowship on a daily basis as well as prophetic insight from other Godly but fallible human beings, are extremely important.

There is a time and a place every day for independent study with other sources like commentaries, notes, dictionaries like Vines, E-Sword, Roberson's Word Pictures and Mounces 2006, etc – but is should not form part of your personal quiet time with God.

In my own life, **outside** my normal quiet time, I usually spend up to 5 hours per day intensively studying the Word, still Spirit led, but also using concordances, dictionaries and other sources. I also love to read autobiographies of Godly men and women, as well as other anointed spiritual books. God uses all of these to build my faith and to give me revelation by the Spirit.

10. God is Spirit and through His Spirit He is fully able to teach you, whether you are an 80-year-old theologian or a 4-year old child, by exactly the same "God is not a respecter of persons" way through the anointing in you (1 John 2:27). From this flows your fellowship with other believers and your outreach to a lost world. As a matter of fact God doesn't want anybody to be lost and go to hell.

Do you eat from the tree of life or the tree of knowledge of good and evil?

11. With the falling into sin of mankind, we have fallen on our heads when we ate from the tree of knowledge of good and evil. We have lost our name and our language (identity in Christ, the Tree of Life) and became far too intellectual – we have relied far too much on our intellectual capacities and our minds: Ezekiel's hard forehead versus Israel's hard forehead and heart.

    Jesus has been crucified on Golgotha (Place of the Scull), and that strongly points to the intellectual fellowship and effort of the Pharisees to understand God intellectually, versus the Holy Spirit who reveals and brings life. Thus there are two kinds of trees: a letter tree of the intellect, and a Spirit Tree of life (Jesus Christ). The Tree of knowledge of good and evil in the garden of Eden, versus the Tree of Life in paradise: Jesus Christ. You make the choice regarding the tree you will feed from; the lead wood in your head, or the Tree of life on the cross wood of your heart?

12. Every time the Holy Spirit quickens a verse, makes it come alive or reveals it to you, you reclaim a portion of your spiritual language and a portion of your Name, of who you are in Christ Jesus. The Word (Spirit-driven and Spirit revealed) is thus absolutely important for the reborn man on soul level (will, thoughts and emotions), because the spirit is impregnated instantaneously (1 Pet 2:24) by God's incorruptable seed (spirit-life salvation). The problem is the narrow/tight birth passage (the narrow road) were the flesh desires against the spirit (Rom 6/7) in your process of rebirth of your soul dimension... through the washing of the water by the Word (Eph 5:26).

Spend time in God's Word, but see to it that you partake in the baptism of the Holy Spirit, for it is only then that His anointing will lead you into a deeper dimension. Without the Holy Spirit, our pastoral workers battle to say anything spiritually relevant from pulpits and elsewhere (Ezek 34). Ezekiel prophesied life into dead bones through the Holy Spirit (Ezek 37:9).

You are a word of God (Isa 55:11). Drink the Word of God so that you, as a word of God, may flow more and manifest His life to others. The Word thus becomes flesh (manifesting itself) in you. As the Word becomes flesh in you more and more, you will find that the Holy Spirit uses more creative ways to communicate, reveal to and teach you – sometimes even in your dreams while you are sleeping:

In a dream, a vision of the night, when deep
sleep falls on men; while they slumber on the bed;
then He opens the ear of men and seals their teaching,
Job 33:15-16

Be sensitive to the prompting of the Spirit in your dreams – write your dreams down immediately as you wake up, and if your dream contained a certain verse or part of Scripture, go to the Word, meditate on it and ask the Holy Spirit to expound it and the meaning of your dream in a deeper Spirit revealed way.

13. Understand and pray Eph 1:18 en 2 Cor 3. Ask a Spirit-filled believer to lay hands on you or do it yourself so that your spiritual eyes and ears can be opened properly (Acts 2), or fall on your face before God under the anointing of the Holy Spirit, in a place of fellowship or corporate worship.

   If Acts 2 means anything, there are two things that do not go together at all: the Holy Spirit moving in and over you, and your dignity. Which one do you choose? Whatever you believe, it can only be the one or the other: life (Holy Spirit) or death (your dignity)? Spiritually speaking, this is definitely true... whether you like it or not. It's in consideration of this fact, and not in offence, that your breakthrough lies.

A stone is a prophetic word released with the sling shot power of the Holy Spirit, penetrating thick skulls of religiosity. –JPF-

Chapter 5

Resources

—ᴍ—

God works in the one waiting upon Him.

God works in the one that waits upon Him. Therefore we should trust the Holy Spirit right from the start. He is powerful enough to teach you because the same power that raised Jesus from the dead, works through Him, and should be flowing through us.

Use only your Bible during your quiet time, and use other books and sources sparingly only to supplement and confirm what the Holy Spirit has already revealed to you.

Answer the following questions to give you more insight into your own Bible-reading habits:

	True	False
I have used only one Bible my whole life.	☐	☐
My Bible is spotless, with little or no writing.	☐	☐
I don't write in my Bible, because I respect it as the Word of God.	☐	☐

If you have answered one or more of these questions in the affirmative, it is time to view and use your Bible in a totally new and fresh way.

Never pick up your Bible without picking up your pen as well, and come to the Word of God full of expectation that He will reveal something new and awesome to you through His Holy Spirit. Fathers like to feed their children from the feastly tables of their hearts.

Make notes in your Bible. Numerous known faith giants knew and experienced the worth of writing in and using their Bibles to jot down their revelations, etc. Take a lesson from them and start writing in your Bible. Leave a precious legacy for your children and grandchildren, like many Godly men and women did.

Take up your pen and charge the ink on the paper in your Bible – it is only letters on paper until it starts to transform your thoughts and help you to grow spiritually to the full stature of Jesus Christ (Eph 4:13). Fully trust the Holy Spirit, and not yourself, to guide you and teach you. In other words, charge the kingdom with the gentle force of the Holy Spirit and your pen.

The following resources can be utilised during your quiet time:

1. A journal or diary to take notes and measure two aspects:
   - What did you read?
   - What was the revelation you received?

2. A writing pen, and two or more in different colours, e g red/black/green.

3. Markers in different colours.

4. A good reference dictionary e g 1828 Noah Webster using a Biblical base to explain word meanings – also available on E-sword (*http://www.e-sword.net/*), a free electronic Bible. Many people can benefit by broadening their vocabulary and comprehension in order to understand not just the literal, but also figurative and spiritual meanings of words like shepherd, tree, oil, ect.

I prefer the Modern King James or the Afrikaanse Old Translation with cross references, as the language is purer, although sometimes not as clear. This necessarily requires more concentration and reliance on the Holy Spirit to receive revelation, and thus more transformation of your mind, than would be the case with some easier or more user-friendly translations. "Easy come easy go" ... An athlete exerting him or herself and putting in much extra exercise and effort in order to reach the winning-post, will taste the breakthrough and victory more rapidly, than one viewing it as just another training session. The same can be said concerning our spiritual growth and breakthroughs.

I also enjoy reading the Amplified Bible or The Message, as well as other translations, for more depth and referencing.

Human beings usually rely on their intellect, but God's sword of the Spirit (Eph 6:13) is the Spirit-driven Word that quickens and brings life.

Chapter 6

The Holy Spirit

—⁓—

There is nothing as strong as softness; nothing as soft as true strength. - St Francis De Sales -

The Holy Spirit is our Teacher, Helper and Councillor. When we quiet down and listen, we will hear the soft voice of the Holy Spirit (see included notes on Hearing God's voice).

"And He said, Go forth and stand on the mountain before Jehovah. And, behold, Jehovah passed by, and a great and strong wind tore the mountains, and broke the rocks in pieces before Jehovah. But Jehovah was not in the wind. And after the wind was an earthquake, but Jehovah was not in the earthquake. And after the earthquake was a fire, but Jehovah was not in the fire. And after the fire was a still, small voice."
1Ki 19:11-12

Although it is a soft voice, the power that is locked up in it, and the power that will flow through us and out of us when we are obedient is awesome.

Christ's soft yoke is the awe-inspiring power which wants to flow with so much grace through you and me, if you can only believe and allow it to flow! It's Fire and Fragrance - if Jesus is the fragrance, the Holy Spirit is the fire that stirs up the fragrance in us, so that people may expierience Jesus.

1. Start with the most important, and pray and ask the Holy Spirit to open your spiritual eyes and ears and to come and teach you and lead you into the mysteries of God.

2. Get things straightened and sorted out now, what is your focus: legalism, nations, people, your flesh or intellect, or is Jesus your only focus?

3. Read and meditate on the following key Scriptures: John 1:1, Eph 6:17, Heb 1, Heb 12:1, Heb 13:13, Heb 4:12, Heb 12:22, 1 John 2:27 and Rev 19:13.

4. Do as Andrew Murray said: if you get the feeling that you are not receiving revelation, or nothing is opening up – then read the verse 3 x with focus and attention; till the light (the daybreak, the Morningstar, Jesus) the sunlight rises in your spirit, and your spiritual eye starts looking beyond your flesh eye of the intellect, deeper into the dimensions of God's heart. God is Spirit (1 John 4); therefore His Word can only be explained/quickened by the Spirit (1 Cor 2).

5. The putting together or stringing together of one verse to another and books in the Bible is of importance in order to understand context. Allow the Holy Spirit to reveal other Scriptures which join together with the portion that you are reading. In that manner the glorious riches of God's Word will be unlocked,

and you will start to see the golden thread of Jesus Christ right throughout the Word, as well as how it applies practically to your life.

Be open to obey the Holy Spirit 100%, even if it seems unconventional. God is a God of new and exciting things and He will often surprise you, based on the unchangable but often hidden truths in His Word.

One day I opened my Bible spontaneously and saw that I had opened at the Index /Contents page of my Bible. Instead of immediately turning to another part of Scripture, like most believers would have done, I remained open and teachable and asked the Holy Spirit to reveal what He wanted to teach me

To put it in a nutshell, what was revealed to me that day is that the whole of Scripture, from Genesis right through the law, prophets, gospels, and epistles to Revelation, has been fulfilled in Jesus Christ, and now the fullness of this Word that has been implanted by God in our hearts and minds, is ready to be manifested in and through us.

I was astounded at the depth and riches of this revelation concerning the compilation of the Bible and the lessons to be learnt from it. If I had fallen back on my conventional thinking, I would have missed out on this revelation and an important aspect of God's character.

6. Ask yourself the following question: How does this Scripture apply to my life? This practical application and meaning in your own life is very important – thereby God wants to teach and help <u>you</u> to grow.

Everyone who has the mighty wind of the Holy Spirit in him , moves forward in power, even while sleeping.
-Brother Lawrence-

7. All of us can improve our reading tecnique and concentration. Read in the following manner, by using your intellectual properties, moving from the outer court, to the inner court and to the Holy of Holies, Spirit led throne room revelation:

- Read thoughtfully,
- repeatedly,
- patiently,
- selectively,
- prayerfully (pray in the Spirit),
- imaginatively,
- meditatively (like David in the night watches),
- focussed, or with focus
- responsive and with a teachable spirit,
- telescopically ... an eagle sees detail and the whole when it seeks outs it prey .[14]

8. Be on the lookout for the following :

- Things that are emphasised like "Verily, verily" or "I say unto you". These phrases are only uttered in the New Testament by Jesus himself and almost always together. The words "verily verily" is used by John, the disciple of love, reflecting the truth dimension of love.
  According to John 8:32 the truth will set you free - not love, although truth in its essence is Godly love which differs vastly from human love. God loves everybody, but most people still

go to hell because they don't want to accept truth as expounded by John in his second and third epistle. His first letter reflected more on God's love.

It is interesting that only John, who loved Him and is described as the disciple of love, would be able to hear Jesus say these profound words. The phrase "Verily, verily I say unto you..." are only to be found in the gospel of John. Peter in his epistle (1 Pet 4:10-11) says let your words be like God's words and Solomon in Prov 25:11 says a word fitly spoken is like apples of gold in pictures of silver. Love, wisdom, truth... It is worth considering these example setting words of Jesus. When last did you say anything near to those words concerning God's Word?

- Things that are repeated often, for example Ezekiel ("child of " or "son of man" or "speak and say")
- Subjects grouped together (such as God is Love, Spirit, Peace, etc)
- Synonyms and antonyms
- Real-life situations
- The whole or the big picture.

There are certain more visible Spirit words for the discerning heart, golden thread words and powerful shadow types in God's Word, for example wine, oil, head, blood, bread, Word. Make sure that you start to define them and ask the Holy Spirit to help you in seeing and identifying with these words in terms of their Old to New Testament shadow types of Jesus. They will help you with the Christological understanding of the Word.

Do you really rely on and trust the Holy Spirit? In reality, how big is God in comparison to yourself? Do you really think He is in a position to teach you when you sit at His feet, or do you stil rely too much on others?

One day, God through His Holy Spirit gave me 10 specific questions to consider during one of my quiet times spent with Him, saying that if I want to discover who I am, I should try and answer the ten questions. He also taught me the order they should be answered. God is a God of detail and even the smallest detail, though it may seem insignificant to you, like the order, has rhythm and meaning. This wonderful revelation led to my writing the book So Who Are You Anyway?

Being insensitive or disobedient to the Holy Spirit that day, would have been a shame and I would have missed a wonderful opportunity for God to bless me personally and to share a part of God's heart with the world. What part of God's heart has the Holy Spirit been trying to reveal to you in order to bless you and others?

I ask again: Do you really rely upon and trust the power and the wisdom of the Holy Spirit to teach you Himself when reading your Bible?

Start with a cheap translation with cross referencing and believe, trust, work in faith and in faith, sweat a little with the help of our Helper. "Application through supplication" How hungry and thirsty are you for God / Jesus / His Word? Be transformed in order to conform to the mind and image of Christ by the Power of the Holy Spirit.

It is wonderful to experience breakthroughs. Remember, Jesus had already paid the price on the cross (It is finished!) You must only pay a time price, everything else is a gift, a free gift from Abba's hands, who through His Word (Jesus) reveals His fulness to us.

You are, so to speak, being reborn into your new identity. "The born identity, reborn right into Christ, not into this world, but into the Kingdom of God."

(See my book *So Who Are You Anyway?*)

Remember:

> ***"It's a journey on the long haul.***
> ***You will be much fuller in***
> ***10 years if you drink daily."***
> *- J P Fourie -*

Chapter 7

Let Us Learn How

—m—

A Spirit-filled believer can see right into the heavenlies.
Dwight L Moody

1. Let's read the following verse, Revelation 19:10b and ask the Holy Spirit to reveal it to us:

   "...Worship God, for the testimony of Jesus is the spirit of prophecy."

   - What does this verse command us?
   To worship God.

   Let's look closer at the word **testimony**.

   - What is the meaning of the word **testimony**?
   It is proof or a verbal report of something. When we tell others about something that happened to us in a spiritual sense, we call it a testimony as you testify verbally or by writing about something that has happened. At the same time it also testifies of God's working in our lives.

- What is the **testimony** of Jesus according to this verse?
  The spirit of prophecy.

- What other verse comes to mind regarding **testimony**?
  Revelation 12:11 that states that you will overcome by the blood of the Lamb and the word of your testimony.

- What does the phrase **word of your testimony** mean?
  It means to tell someone about something that God has done for you personally. It also means to declare with boldness that you are a believer and to tell somebody about your faith.

- What is your most recent testimony, and with whom did you share it? Summarize and write it here.

  ....

  ....

  ....

  ....

  ....

  ....

  ....

Dig a little deeper: As I like to testify about Jesus, the word of my testimony is Jesus, the Word of God! (Author)

Let us look at **word.**

- Which verse immediately comes to mind?
  - ➤ John 1 says the following:
    In die beginning was the Word and the Word was with God and the Word was God.

  - ➤ Revelation 19:13 says that Jesus' Name is the Word of God.

Let's take the word **prophecy.**

- What explanation does 1 Cor 14:3 give for prophecy?
  It says to prophesy is to build up, exhort and comfort somebody.

- What does Moses say in Numbers 11:29 of prophets?
  "Would God that all Jehovah's people were prophets, that Jehovah would put His Spirit upon them!"

Thus, when we read the Bible Christologically, we take the Name of Jesus as a powerful form of testimony and prophetic proclamation over people, situations, disease, etc.

- When was the last time you prophesied over some-body, i e you built somebody up, exhorted or comforted them?

....

....

....

....

- To whom will you prophesy today? Ask the Holy Spirit to give you the name of the person as well as a prophetic word that will bless him/her. Write it down. (How about your children?)

....

....

....

....

....

....

....

....

....

Now be bold, and release the word to the person.

- What are the situations and/or problems in your own life over which the Name of Jesus should be proclaimed today? Write it down and then proclaim it audible:

LORD, today I proclaim the Name of Jesus Christ

over ....

....

....

....

....

....

....

....

and prophesy in the death defying resurrection power that flows through Him and through me, a Godly intervention and breakthrough regarding this situation. In the Name of Jesus Christ, Amen.

Allow the Holy Spirit, through the sword, which is the Word of God (Heb 4:12), to guide you to truth and more revelation... Let the streams of living water of the Spirit well up within you!

There is a divine golden thread right through the Word of God that is repeated in different ways to the eater of honey and the drinker of the sweeter wine. This takes place so that the depths of God can be revealed through Jesus Christ, the Spirit of prophesy, and the Holy Spirit revealing Him to us...until the stream of living water wells up within you and flows out through your mouth!

2. Let's take another verse, Mark 13:28, and trust the Holy Spirit to guide and teach us:

> *"And learn the parable of*
> *the fig-tree: when her branch*
> *is still tender and puts*
> *out leaves, you know*
> *that summer is near."*

- When does the branch of a fig-tree grow tender?
  It is a sign of new growth and readiness to bear fruit.

- Where does a fig-tree bear its fruit?
  A fig-tree bears its fruit only on its new growth.
  Spiritually speaking this is a sign of spiritual revival and has nothing to do with specific nations. It is my view that, at most, it may point to the hearts of Jews becoming soft and receptive and thus point to their salvation on a large scale, so becoming part of the new Jerusalem spoken about in Heb 12:22. It is thus indicative of their return to Jesus Christ and the heavenly Jerusalem, already being built by God for the past 2000 years, and does not signify human temples built with stone.
  This is a spiritual return to God that is Spirit, and not a physical nation returning to a physical country

or geographical area: the territory of Spiritual Israelites is much larger than a small piece of desert in the Middle East (Gal 4:24) – therefore the Word says:

"Make the place of your tent larger, and let them stretch out the curtains of your dwellings. Do not spare, lengthen your cords and strengthen your stakes; "(Isa 54:2), because

The earth is Jehovah's, and the fullness of it; the world, and those who dwell in it. (Ps 24:1).

There is *neither Greek nor Jew, circumcision and uncircumcision, foreigner, Scythian, slave or freeman, but Christ is all things in all.* (Col 3:11), after the veil, which is the flesh of Jesus, has been torn. Now there is only one new man in Christ and one body.

- When does spiritual revival take place?

It takes place when wrong thinking and religious leaven that *leavens all the lump,* (Gal 5:9) disappear from the body (believers) of Jesus Christ.

The religious crowd was and today still is the greatest enemy of Jesus: the scribes and Pharisees that believed in their traditions and the dead letter of the Mosaic law, but would not believe in the Living Word, Jesus Christ. Man should always remain receptive to the Holy Spirit and maintain a teachable spirit. This will allow the Spirit to confront and deal with dead religious rules and traditions in your own life. Then only can you focus purely on Jesus Christ, the Author and Finisher of our faith, through the Word, and by the Holy Spirit.

He washed the feet of the disciples so that we will have feet *shod with the preparation of the gospel of peace (Eph 6), so that His enemies can be trampled upon while He sits at the right hand of the Father, until He returns to meet His* ruling and reigning bride (body) at the wedding feast, a bride married to a King that rules and reigns here on earth.

We find another reference to fig leaves at the beginning of the Bible when Adam and Eve tried to conceal their sin and nakedness with leaves from the fig-tree:

And the eyes of both of them were opened.
And they knew that they were naked.
And they sewed fig leaves together and
made girdles for themselves. Gen 3:7

Do not try to hide your sin as Adam and Eve did – be honest and receptive to God and people, without the fig-tree leaves of sin consciousness.

We should have a God consciousness. Do not focus on the self and my little sin and unrighteousness, but repent earnestly and start to focus on Jesus (Heb 12:1-2), and everything that is good within yourself (Phil 1:6). Be quick to repent in childlike faith and thus maintain a God consciousness and not a self or sin consciousness.

If your heart condemns you, God is greater than your heart (1 John 3:20), and only they that are pure in heart will see God (Matt 5:8). Therefore strive towards an uncontaminated pure childlike faith in God, and not perfectionism, legalism or a type of spiritual autism!

And they heard the voice of Jehovah God
walking in the garden in the cool of the day.
And Adam and his wife hid themselves
from the presence of Jehovah God
in the middle of the trees of the garden.
And Jehovah God called to Adam
and said to him, Where are you?
Gen 3:8-9

Can you hear God calling you to stand, through the rent veil of the body of Jesus Christ, absolutely naked and without shame before Him (transparent, for and before the King of kings)? And when joy unspeakable bubbles up in you, to break out, like David did, in undignified dancing, and jubilation and praises before Him as never before - drunk with love and full of the sweet wine of the Holy Spirit, and still craving more. Mindless or out of your mind, and limping (like Jacob) (having been hit on your head and with your spiritual eyes and ears wide open and responsive)... - not relying on the so-called strongest muscle in your body anymore, for when you are weak, He can be strong!

David was a man after God's own heart (Act 13:22). His heart and motives were pure, and even when he sinned in a major way, he was quick to repent and to say : "Sorry Lord, I have sinned again ... please forgive me."

So take off you fig-tree leaves of sin consciousness and become drunk, filled with the Holy Spirit wine in the tent of David... and worship and minister unto God 24 hours a day, 7 days a week! Noah made his own wine and drank it, and lay naked before his sons who were ashamed of him, and tried to cover up his nakedness. Michal, Saul's daughter and David's wife, also despised David when he, girded with a linen ephod, danced with all his might before God. Just like David you should be able to dance without shame, and to be filled and drunk with the new wine of the Holy Spirit. Just before His ascension, Jesus declared that he will not drink of this fruit of the vine, until that day when He drinks it new with us in His Father's kingdom. (Matt 26:29)

As the head of His body, He invites us to "Come and drink" – not come and think! He sent the Spirit to fill our new wineskins with the new wine, when the power (baptism and repeated infilling) of the Holy Spirit ascends on us with tongues of fire to burn away all religious leaven in us.

When the fig tree, first individually, and then collectively start bearing the fruit of the Spirit: righteousness, peace, joy unspeakable and full of glory – you will know that you have been filled! And when people want to throw a cloth over your nakedness (like Noah) because they are ashamed of your free (where the Spirit of the Lord is, there is liberty), undignified worship of the King of Kings and the Lord of Lords, the second coming of the King of Kings is at hand, in you as well as to the Body! Undignified, free worship of the Lord will demolish all religious demons and will facilitate the powerful flowing of the anointing. Nakedness = open unselfish admiration and receptiveness.

Therefore, Sons and Daughters, let it flow freely, release it so that the King of Glory can come in - in you, and in His body! Bring Him back through your naked unadulterated worship and adoration of the Father, the Son, and the Holy Spirit!

Also study and meditate the following verses concerning the **fig tree**:

- *Judges 9:10-11:*

*And the trees said to the **fig tree**, You come and reign over us. But the **fig tree** said to them, Should I forsake my sweetness and my good fruit, and go to be promoted over the trees?*

- *Song of Solomon 2:13*

*… the **fig tree** puts forth her green figs, and the vines with the tender grape give a good smell. Arise, My love, My beautiful one, and come away.*

- *Hosea 2:12*

*And I will destroy her vines and her **fig trees**, of which she has said, They are my rewards that my lovers have given me.*

- *Joel 1:12*

*The vine is dried up, and the **fig tree** droops, the pomegranate and the palm tree, and the apple tree; all the trees of the field are dried up, because joy has dried up from the sons of men.*

Where is the "joy unspeakable and full of glory" worship of which the Spirit testified through me?

- *Joel 2:22*

Do not be afraid, beasts of the field; for the pastures
of the wilderness grow green; for the tree bears
its fruit, and the fig tree and the vine yield their strength.

- *Mat 21:19*

...And seeing a fig tree in the way, He came to it and found
nothing on it except leaves only. And He said to it, let
no fruit grow on you forever.
And immediately the fig tree withered away.

- *Mat 21:21*

Jesus answered and said to them, Truly I say to you,
If you have faith and do not doubt, you shall not only do
this miracle of the fig tree, but also; if you shall
say to this mountain, Be moved and be thrown
into the sea; it shall be done.

- *Mar 11:21*

And Peter, remembering, said to Him,
Rabbi, behold, the fig tree which You
cursed has withered away.

Read this verse with Gal 5:1... Can you or religious leaven give life back to this tree? Only the Spirit can supply the true early and late figs of spiritual revival!

- *Luke 13:6-7*

> *He also spoke this parable: A certain man had a*
> ***fig tree*** *planted in his vineyard. And he came and*
> *sought fruit on it, and found none. And he said*
> *to the dresser of his vineyard, Behold, these*
> *three years I come seeking fruit on this*
> ***Fig tree****, and find none. Cut it down,*
> *why does it encumber the ground?*

Let the Word speak to you, through the resurrection power of the Holy Spirit while quickening your inner man with every verse – no dead letter upon dead letter, precept upon precept, but Sword Word upon Sword Word, in the Holy Name of Jesus Christ, the Son of God, the Firstborn among many, that calls you His brother and His friend – "He ain't heavy, He is my brother." Spring up, o well, from deep within me – Spirit-driven anointed Sword Word of God!

3. Now it is your turn to trust the Holy Spirit to teach you.

   Pray and ask the Holy Spirit to open your spiritual eyes and ears, as well as your heart so that you will hear His voice clearly:

   Let us take the first verse of the loved and well-known Psalm 23:

   > *"The LORD is my Shepherd;*
   > *I shall not want."*

- Ask the Holy Spirit to reveal to you the meaning of the word shepherd in this context. Write down all thoughts flowing through you:

....

....

....

....

....

....

....

....

....

....

....

- Now ask the Holy Spirit to reveal other relevant Scriptures concerning the word shepherd, and write it down.

....

....

....

....

....

....

The importance of first and foremost receiving your revelation from only the Holy Spirit, can not be over-emphasized. If you use other books and references prematurely, without first trusting 100% in the power of the Holy Spirit to guide and teach you, you will immediately fall back to relying on your intellect and the revelations of others. Thereafter you will find it difficult to hear the voice of the Holy Spirit clearly. Decide today if you trust the Holy Spirit enough to teach and guide you.

- What does Jesus tell Peter in John 21 concerning love, lambs and sheep?

....

....

....

....

....

- What does God tell Ezekiel in Ezek 34 with regard to **shepherds**?

....

....

....

....

....

....

....

• Who is your **shepherd**, ie who takes care of you and protect you?

....

....

....

....

....

• What does this verse promise you personally?

....

....

....

....

....

- What need do you currently experience in your personal life, eg happiness, financial provision, employment, health, partner, an unsaved loved one, ect?

....

....

....

....

....

....

....

- Pray out loud now and remind God (according to Isa 62:6-7) of His promise here in Ps 23. Then ask Him to provide the needs mentioned above.

- Don't you think all of us are shepherds to a certain degree? Why?

....

....

....

....

....

- How can you be a shepherd today – what specific actions are you planning today in order to be a shepherd like Jesus?:
    - o   In your family

    ....

    ....

    ....

    ....

    ....

    ....

    ....

    - o   At work

    ....

    ....

    ....

    ....

    ....

    ....

    ....

o   In the body of Christ or among your friends

....

....

....

....

....

....

o   Towards people crossing your path, e g your
    neighbour, or a stranger passing by, etc

....

....

....

....

....

....

Only at this stage, after you have allowed the Holy
Spirit to guide and teach you, should you use other references and books to further meditate and investigate the
meaning of **shepherd**:

- What is the meaning of **shepherd** in the dictionary?

  ....

  ....

  ....

  ....

  ....

  ....

  ....

  ....

- What explanation does a concordance like Vines, Strongs, etc offer?

  ....

  ....

  ....

  ....

  ....

  ....

  ....

....

....

....

....

- Also read the following explanation given by Easton to realise how special and precious you are to God:

> *"The duties of a shepherd in an unenclosed country like Palestine were very onerous. In early morning he led forth the flock from the fold, marching at its head to the spot where they were to be pastured. Here he watched them all day, taking care that none of the sheep strayed, and if any for a time eluded his watch and wandered away from the rest, seeking diligently till he found and brought it back. In those lands sheep require to be supplied regularly with water, and the shepherd for this purpose has to guide them either to some running stream or to wells dug in the wilderness and furnished with troughs. At night he brought the flock home to the fold, counting them as they passed under the rod at the door to assure himself that none were missing. Nor did his labours always end with sunset. Often he had to guard the fold through the dark hours from the attack of wild beasts, or the wily attempts of the prowling thief."*[15]

This is how the Father feels about you!

Chapter 8

Spirit Words

—ww—

*Call unto me, and I will answer thee, and will show thee
great things, and difficult, which thou knowest not.*
Jer 33:3

When you allow the Holy Spirit to lead and teach you,
you discover the riches and depths of God's Word,
as never before. Then you will discover the shadow types,
typology, symbolism and Christology in everything you
read, see and experience and you will begin to understand
the language of the Bible, not only on an intellectual level,
but most of all on a life changing spiritual level.

Ordinary words, names of places, first names and
figures will get literal and spiritual meaning, and God's
Word, Jesus Christ will literally and spiritually open up
before you. God himself invites us in the Old Testament to
call upon Him, and He promises that He will make known
to us great and difficult things which we know not. Jesus
confirms this in the New Testament when He promises the
following:

"But the Comforter, even the Holy Spirit,
whom the Father will send in my name,
he shall teach you all things, and bring to
your remembrance all that I said unto you."
John 14:26

Let us together discover the awesome wonder of God's Word by looking and considering a few Spirit words. Although slightly altered and added to as lead by the Holy Spirit, the following way of understanding and revealing the symbolic Christological meaning of words in the Bible, comes from the heart and pen of Dr Kelley Varner in his two books named *Understanding Types, Shadows, and Names, Vol 1 and 2*[16] of a series that will be published semi annually.

Eagle

Spiritual: The Conqueror or Overcomer; Resurrection; Heavenly things

Corner stones: Deut 32:11-12, Ps 103:5,
Is 40:31, Ezek 1:10,14 Eph 1:3;
2:6; Rev 3:21

Literal: 32 x in the Bible (MKJV)

Eagles are king amongst all birds. The majestic golden eagle which derives its name from its golden crown which becomes more evident with maturity) builds its nest in high rocky cliffs and has a wing span of 2-3 m. Eagles mate for life. Both parents sit on the nest and take care of the young ones. They are first taught to stand and then to fly. At first the parents will carry the young ones on their backs whilst flying, until the little one is strong enough to fly on its own. Eagles are very discerning about what they will eat, and because of their excellent vision (8 times better than a human being), eagles can choose their prey.

Eagles can see a storm coming and soar above the rain and wind...in fact it uses the wind. Eagles can effortlessly stay in the air for hours on end, by floating on air currents with almost no movement of its wings. Eagles renew their strength and youthful appearance by shedding their feathers and have a long life span (20 – 30 years in nature).The eagle's biggest enemy is the snake or serpent

.
Hebrew: *nesher (Strongs #5404) : to tear apart, eagle or
other big bird of prey*

Greek: *aetos (Strongs #105): eagle; from root aer :*
wind

Jesus Christ

Jesus Christ is the Son of God, the majestic King of
the air, the conqueror who has overcome the enemy, even
triumphed over death (1 Cor 15:55-58; Rev 3:21). To Him
is given all power in heaven and on the earth (Mat 28:18).
By conquering all powers and pricipalities, He gained the
victory and now sits in heavenly places (Eph 1:20-21). Jesus
Christ is the Good Shepherd, who carries us, His lambs and
sheep (Is 40:11) like an eagle parent (Deut 32:11-12), and
lovingly cares and feeds us.

Faith in Action

Christians who are partakers in the Godly nature, and a
heavenly calling, have been seated in heavenly places with
Christ (Eph 1:3, 3:10). We have the authority in Jesus' Name
(Mark 6:15-20) and should soar like eagles above earthly
problems and situations.

Eagle Christians should live as follows:

"... but they that wait for Jehovah shall renew their
strength; they shall mount up with wings as eagles; they
shall run, and not be weary; they shall walk, and not faint.
Isa 40:31

Ps 91 describes the safe haven or "nest " and protection
of eagle Christians, and in Ps 103, we are promised that He
will satisfy our desires with good things, *so that* our youth is
renewed like the eagle. Eagle Christians know the wind of
the Holy Spirit and use it to soar and glide effortlessly above
the worries of this world (John 3:8, Rom 8:14). Just as is the
case with the eagle, our biggest enemy is the serpent satan
(spelt with lower case because he has been defeated), but we

don't have to fear him because we already have the power to trample on "snakes and scorpions", insignificant little monsters with large masticators (speaking of legalism)(Luke 10:19)

Deeper into the golden ore of the Word

Ex. 19:4; Lev 11:13; Deut 14:12; 28:49; 32:11; 1 Sam 25:6; 2 Sam 1:23; Job 9:26; Ps 103:5; Prov 23:5; 30:17, 19; Isa 40:31; Jer 4:13; 13:21; 31:8; 48:40; 49:16, 22; Lam 4:19; Ezek 1:10; 10:14; 17:3, 6, 7; Dan 4:33; 7:4; Hos 8:1; Obad 1:4; Micah 5:3; Hab 1:8; Rev 4:7; 12:14;

Blood

Spiritual: Life, Cleansing, Forgiveness, Atonement, Reconciliation

Corner stones: Lev 17:11; Mat 26:28, 1 Cor 10:16; Heb 9:12,22; 1 Pet 1:18-20; Rev 1:5

Literal: 446 x in Bible (MKJV)

Under the old order, or the Old Testament, the blood of an animal was used for reconciliation and cleansing of sin – thus an animal was used as a scapegoat.

In the New Testament the blood of Jesus is the sacrifice.

Hebrew: *dam (Strong's #1818) blood when poured out, causes death in man and animal. Also refer to the juice of grapes; figuritively bloodletting (blooddrops).*

Jesus Christ

Jesus' blood cleansed us from sin and unrighteousness (Rev 5:1). He is the Passover Lamb (Exo 12:13, 1 Cor 5:7) crucified for us, and by believing in His blood, there is grace and salvation (Rom 3:25). In the Garden of Gethsemane, Jesus prayed and wrestled so fervently that his sweat became like huge drops of blood (Luk 22:44).

After His crucifiction one of the soldiers pierced His side with a spear and blood and water issued forth (John 19:34). Jesus himself told His disciples in Mat 26:28: " ...for this is My blood of the covenant, which is poured out for many unto remission of sins. "

Faith in Action

Life is in the blood, says Moses in Lev 17:11. As believers we have been bought through the precious blood of the Lamb, Jesus Christ, set free, righteous and sanctified (Rom 5:9; Heb 13:12, 1 Pet 1:18-19), and now we have eternal life (John 3:16). With Communion, the wine is the sign of Jesus' precious blood. As Christians, we can now boldly go to the throne of grace, by the blood of Jesus Christ (Heb 10:19; 13:20).

Deeper into the golden ore of the Word

Gen. 4:10, 11; 9:4-6; 37:22, 31; 42:22; Ex. 12, Lev. 3:13, 17; 4:5-7, Deut 32:42-43; Josh 2:19; 1 King 2:9, Joel 2:30, 31; Matt 27:4, 24-25; Mark 14:24; Luke 11:50-51; John 6:53-56; Act 1:19, 17:26; 20:28; 1 Cor 11:25-30; Col 1:14, 20; Heb 2:14; 9:7-14, 18-25; 10:4, 19, 29; 11:28; 12:24; 1 Pet 1:2, 1 John 5:8; Rev 7:14; 11:6; 12:11; 19:13.

Dead Sea / Salt Sea

Spiritual: Low Point, No flow, No life, Death

Corner Stones: Gen 14:3, Ezek 47:8-11, Joel 2:20, Eph 4:9

Literal: 23 x in the Bible (MKJV)

The Dead Sea or Salt Sea is situated in the South of Palestine on the lowest point on earth – approximately 433 m below sea level, with the effect that water flows in, but nothing flows out, and nothing lives in it.

Hebrew: *Salt originates from melach (Strong's #4417) powder and specific salt as inherent meaning .*

Jesus Christ

Jesus Christ came from heaven to earth and went into the lowest pit of hell (Deut 32:22, Ps 86:13). He humiliated and humbled Himself and was obedient to death so that we, as believers, may have life, and life in abundance (John 10:10, 11:25). He has tasted the salt of death for every human being (Heb 2:9) and thereafter destroyed death through conquering it (1 Cor 15:54). Now believers can declare with Paul:

But if we died with Christ, we believe
that we shall also live with him;
knowing that Christ being raised from the
dead dieth no more; death no more hath
dominion over him.
Rom 6:8-9

*For the law of the Spirit of life in Christ Jesus
made me free from the law of sin and of death.*
Rom 8:2

Faith in action

Jesus has saved us from death – people that are still dead in their sin, lives in dry places, a landscape of salt where God is not. As present believers, we must flow (Joh 7:38) and grow against this mainstream lakes of death. What we take in through the Holy Spirit must of necessity gush out of us in streams of living water to bring life to others.

When we say no to the Holy Spirit when He wants to touch certain areas of our lives and cleanse it with His all consuming fire, those places will stay sick, and be delivered over for salt, as Ezekiel says (Ezek 47:11). As believers we are not entitled to look back and crave after worldly things like Lot's wife did. Jesus says in Luke 9:62 "No one having put his hand to the plow and looking back, is fit for the Kingdom of God." If we look back spiritually we would change into salt pillars, and be of no value to the Gospel (Gen 19:26).

This is the general state in which 90 % of the Westernised institutionalised "church" finds itself today – very little life flowing out of a dead sea of religiosity.

Deeper into the golden ore of the Word

Gen 14:3, Num 34:3,12, Deut 3:17, Jos. 3:16; 12:3; 15:2, 5; 18:19; Ezek 47, Amos 8:12, Rom 5:10-21, 8:6, Eph 5:14, Col 1:18, Heb 2:14, Jam 2:20, Rev 1:18.

Esther (Hadassah)

Spiritual: Bride of Christ

Corner Stone: Esther 1-10, Ps 45:9-15,
Eph 5:22-23, Rev 21:1-10

Literal: Esther 56 x in Bible (MKJV)
Bride 15 x in Bible (MKJV)

Hebrew: Esther: *Ecter (Strong's #635)* meaning star, the planet Venus, joy, happiness, secret, hidden, I have been hidden.

Hadassah: Hadaccah (Strong's #1919) feminine of hadac (Strong's #1918) which means myrtle tree. Also jump, jump up, joy, happiness.

Jesus Christ

Jesus Christ is the heavenly Bridegroom, the Sun of righteousness (Mal 4:2). Jesus is seen in the book of Esther as the king for whom His Bride, the Body, prepares herself through the ministry of the Word which is depicted by Mordecai, and the Holy Spirit which is depicted by Hegai (Sword of the Spirit, Eph 6:17).

- The golden sceptre in Est 4:11 symbolically represents Jesus Christ, because to Him belongs all the authority .
- The gallows upon which Haman (our sin and pride heaped on Him) was hung (Est 5:14, 7:9) meaning "tree" points forth to the cross (1 Pet 2:24)
- Jesus is also pictured in the kingly crown (Est 6:8) for He is the King of kings (Rev 19:16)

- The king's ring also symbolically points towards Jesus as the beloved firstborn Son (Hag 2:20-23, Luk 9:35, Luk 15:22)
- Jesus is the heavenly Gift, the Word who became flesh (Joh 1:14, Col 1), and therefore the heavenly "Pur" (portion or part) also has strong Christological meaning.

Faith in action

The body is the "heavenly Jerusalem" (Heb 12:22-23), – she is the Lamb's bride beautified and fully anointed for Him (Rev 21:2,9). Esther was a "star". The Lord placed her in a dark place in order to bring light to help people in looking heavenward and up to God. Exactly like Jesus, so is His Body, a light unto the world (Mat 5:14) and as believers, we focus peoples' attention heavenward, on Jesus Christ (Heb 12:1-2) for we are called to "come up hither" (Rev 4:1).

The myrtle tree is known for its fragrance and beauty and excemplifies cleansing and purification. It has been used to make huts for the feast of tabernacles (Neh 8:15-16). Similarly our bodies and the body of Jesus (body of believers here on earth) is a temple of the Holy Spirit (Eph 2:21-22). The myrtle tree is also one of the seven trees of Is 41:19 – The Body of Christ must experience the "seven Spirits of God" reflecting His fullness. Jesus is the Man amongst the myrtle trees (Sag 1:8-11), and He walks in our midst (Rev 1:13,20).

There is only one bride and that is the anointed Spirit baptised Spirit-filled Body of Christ, who can dance undig-nified and worship Him with all their might, like David did. Maybe 1% of the Body today is truly anointed and without religious leaven – the rest is therefore keeping Jesus from coming back. Get rid of the leaven in your life, get under the anointing, and drunk in the Spirit, thereby hastening the return of the King of glory (Rev 22:20).

Deeper into the golden ore of the Word

Est 2:15-22; 4:5-10; 5:1-7; 7:1-8; 8:1-7; 9:29-32; Isa 49:18, 61:10; Jer 2:32, 7:34, 16:9, 25:10, 33:11; Joel 2:16; Joh 3:29; Rev 21:2,9, 22:17.

Bread

Spiritual: Jesus, and His body, the Living Word of God

Corner stones: Exo 16, Mat 4:3-4, 15:26, Joh 6, 1 Cor 5:7-8, 10:16-17

Literal: 339 x in the Bible (MKJV)

Bread was an important element in Israel's levitical worship. Weekly, 12 loaves of show bread, (unleavened), were baked for the tabernacle and later placed in the temple... unleavened bread in us. There is also the feast of unleavened bread (Exo 13) to celebrate the Exodus out of Egypt - do you want to get out of Egypt?

Hebrew: from lechem (Strong's #3899) = food, mostly bread, or grain (from which it is made).

Greeks: artos (Strong's #740) = bread.

Jesus Christ

Jesus Christ is the Living Bread, the only living Bread, the Bread of God: John 6:51:

I am the living bread which came down out of heaven:
if any man eat of this bread, he shall live for ever:
yea and the bread which I will give is my flesh,
for the life of the world.

Jesus also says that man cannot live from physical bread alone, but of the living Bread, that is His Word (Luke 4:4). In the Lord's Prayer He teaches us to pray for our "daily bread". The bread that Jesus broke at the Last Supper, which we sacramentally maintain as the Holy Communion is symbolic of His body that has been broken on the cross: "and the bread that I shall give, is my flesh which I will give for the life of the world".

The meaning of the word the Lord's Supper or Holy Communion has a religious ritualistic connotation in the minds of most people, and misses the celebratory element of toasting and feasting with the King of kings. I believe Jesus, forever alive, also wants it to be a festive occasion in our normal dinner. Eating bread and drinking a glass of wine or breaking a piece of freshly baked bread, and handing it to your brother or sister next to you and saying: Jesus, we are thinking of You and celebrating You to each other. 1 Cor 11:21 refer to believers who got drunk and gorged them-selves or physical food and alcohol.

This lead to an over reaction erring on the conservative side – being so religious and pious that we don't experi-ence any joy during the Lord's Supper. Paul as it was, was primarily rebuking the Corinthians for their unrighteous behaviour. Verse 28 tells us to test ourselves in this regard and then cross-referencing 2 Cor 13:5 and 1 John 3:6, 20 tells us to meditate upon Christ in us and us in Him, whilst breaking the bread (both physical and the Word (Rev 19:13) and taking the cup. It then becomes nearly impossible not to be joyous, which in its turn brings healing to the bones (Prov 17:22).

In the Old Testament Melchizedek, a shadow type of Jesus Christ (Heb 7:15-17), for the first time ever broke bread and used wine; symbolic of His death on the cross and the Lord's Supper which followed later on (Gen14: 18). God rained manna from heaven "bread from heaven" (Ex.

16:14) – The manna is also symbolic of Jesus Christ who came from heaven to earth, was crucified and resurrected, so that we can live.

Faith in action

When believers celebrate the Lord's supper, we must do it with cleansed hearts, in Spirit and in truth, without any leaven of religion, rules and traditions. We must live from God's bread in exactly the same manner, His Word Jesus Christ - each and every day take a fresh piece to feed our inner man. The manna in the old Testament couldn't be kept for use the following day – it became stale and rotten (Exo 16); God's Word and His mercies are new every morning.

Healing and salvation are the "bread of the children" (Mat 15:26, Mark 7:27). Jesus twice multiplied the bread to feed the people (Joh 6) – in the exact same manner we should sow God's word and speak and use it to feed hungry people – it will never be used up (Luk 15:17). As quickly as you receive it, start sowing it, and God will multiply it, because God is a God of multitude and abundance (John 10:10), a God who provides "Jehovah Jireh". David (1 Sam 21:6) was not afraid to eat the Holy Bread in the Holy place; he had boldness and was a man after God's heart. Like David, believers shouldn't be afraid to "eat" God's Word, Jesus Christ, with boldness, and to live thereof abundantly.

Deeper into the golden ore of the Word

Gen. 3:19; 14:18; Ex. 12:8, 13:6-7, 25:30, Lev 21:8, 23:6, Num 4:7, Deut 8:3, Ruth 2:14, Ps 37:25, 78:25, 127:2, Prov 31:14,27, Isa 4:1, 30:20, 55:1-2, 58:7, Mal 1:7, Luke 4:4, 11:11, John 13:18, Acts 12:3, 1 Cor 11:23-30, 2 Cor 9:10, 2 Thess 3:8, Heb 9:2, Rev 2:17

Note:

When we break bread for many, enough will remain for us to feed of, for we are also bread to be broken, given as a gift to and from His body.

Chapter 9

Points to Ponder

—ɯ—

You would not have found God if He hadn't started looking for you long ago. –Blaise Pascal-

We should all take heed of the following aspects:

1. 2 Cor 3 warns us against the way of the scribes, ie the letter kills, but the Spirit makes alive. We should always rely on the guidance and help of the Holy Spirit in stead of relying on our own intellect and knowledge.

2. In 1 John 2:27 the importance of the anointing is emphasized, as well as the fact that this anointing abides within us and that we should allow the Holy Spirit to teach us.

3. Without the guidance of the Holy Spirit, a strong possibility exist that you could fall victim to searching the Scriptures (Jesus' words in Joh 5:39). Be careful not to search the Scriptures as unbelievers would – you are seeking the face of the only true God, and

thereby you find yourself and your identity in Christ, and not the other way around.

4. Ask the Spirit to expose any leaven of legalism and spirit of religion (Gal 1 and 5). Remember, where the Spirit of the Lord is, there is liberty and total freedom for God to reveal Himself and to freely praise and worship Him with all your might – thus there is no place for even a vestige of religious rules and preconceived ideas.

5. Try not to read the Old Testament in isolation, without reading the New Testament. We live on the right side of the cross; the price has been paid in full. It is thus required that we should read and interpret everything Christologically. Jesus, the golden thread runs right from Genesis 1 to the last verse in Revelation. The moment we loose sight of Jesus and the price He paid, we are in danger of starting to question certain parts in the Bible and are defiling and dishonouring the character of God.

    It's all about your relationship with Him and His life flowing through you and touching other people – Jesus Christ should always be the centre and focus of your quiet time, as He, through the help and guidance of the Holy Spirit is the way, the truth and the life to our Father (Abba).

6. We read our Bibles so that God can reveal Himself to us, communicate personally with each of us, and that our minds can be renewed according to Romans 12:1-2. The main focus should never be to cleverly memorise Scriptures in order to impress other people. It should be:

"To hear better, My child"
"To see better, My child."

So that we can walk in the Spirit with our spiritual eyes and ears open and remain sensitive to the leading and revelation of the Holy Spirit. Our relationship is with the living Almighty God and His life flows through us.

7. "It is all about Jesus, not about you."

8. There are three levels for reading the Bible (1 Thes 5:23):

    a. **Spiritual level** (Holy of Holies): Does your Spirit respond when you read Bible as depicted in Ps 42? *Deep calleth unto deep.* On this level you allow the Holy Spirit to speak the Word through you and to reveal it to you. The Spirit quickens and brings life, but the letter kills, and according to 2 Cor 3 the Spirit transforms us from one degree of glory to the glory and full stature of Jesus Christ.

    b. **Soul level**: (Inner Court) On this level you hear and speak the Word and allow it to transform your mind through the water (bath) of the Word (Rom 12:1-2, Eph 5:26). But there is still no deep communication between the Holy Spirit and your spirit, and limited life changing revelation.

    c. **Carnal level**: (Outer Court)Usually reading the Bible on this level is just a ritual or habit in which you search the Scriptures, but with little or no effect and change, because the letter kills and it simply becomes another set of morality rules.

Paul had to fall from his "high horse" of religion and was blinded to tradition, legalism, leaven of the Scribe sort by the glorious brilliant light of Jesus Christ for a few days so that his spiritual eyes and ears could be opened. God's thoughts are higher than our thoughts (Isa 55) and His ways are not our ways, and therefore He invites us "to come up hither" (Rev 4:1, 11:12). That means we should look at people and events with God's eyes, and stay away from human, carnal criticism, judgement and opinions. Any form of racism saddens God and the Holy Spirit and deprives you of Spirit-driven revelation... so examine your heart closely if you have a hunger for revelation knowledge.

Balaam's ass had to speak to him to enable him to see and hear the angel of the LORD. Peter, John and James were uneducated men, Luke a medical doctor, and Paul a Pharisee, but all of them had to get their mind and intellect out of the way, before they could use it in the right way to grow in the grace and truth of our Lord Jesus Christ (2 Petr 3:18).

He is the Head and we are the feet (His body) – therefore He washed the feet, and not the head of His disciples and thus ours too. Mary Magdelene anointed His head with oil (Mat 26:7). So come and drink from Him and forget the intellectual dissecting kind of thinking – He invites us to "Come and drink," and not to "Come and think" (John 4:13-14).

Meditate upon His Word with your spiritual eyes (enlightened eyes of your understanding) and do not rely on your wonderful intellect. In comparison with

God, the 4-10% of your and my brains we utilise, seems insignificant and that of an idiot. The only way you can "understand" and enjoy the depths of God is through your spirit or the eyes of your heart, by the Holy Spirit.

You should always ask yourself the following question: How do I read the Bible? Do I come to drink (Rev 22:17, revelation knowledge), or do I come to think (letter knowledge)?

My prayer for you is that God wil grant you the Spirit of wisdom and revelation in knowledge of Him, enlightened eyes of your understanding, so that you may know what is the hope of His calling, and what is of the glory of His inheritance in the saints (Eph 1:18).

"Father, in the Name of Jesus and in the
death defying power of the Holy Spirit,
I pray that the spiritual eyes and ears of this
reader now be opened and that awesome
revelation knowlegde will be his/her daily portion,
because of his/her desire to have a living personal rela-
tionship with You, the living God. Amen."

Chapter 10

A Last Word

—ᜠ—

The Spirit of the One who raised
up Jesus from the dead dwells in you. (Rom 8:11)

The same Spirit of the One who raised Jesus from the dead, dwells in all of us, provided we are washed in the blood and baptized with the Holy Spirit. God is no respecter of persons. This same power now works through us as temples of the Holy Spirit.

Guidelines, resources, recommendations, and tecniques should never ever hinder the flow and freedom of the Holy Spirit. It always is and should be a two-way discussion if you want to feel God's power flowing through you, and not just acquiring more intellectual knowledge that you share with others. Are your words like prophetic words that build up, exhort and comfort others? Can you honestly say that your words are like God's words, as stated in 1 Petr 4:10-11? Or that you speak the right words at the right time which are like golden apples on a silver tray as Solomon said in Proverbs 25:11?

The baptism of the Holy Spirit, with which Jesus baptises, and the receiving of your Spirit tongue in order to bypass (subdue) your intellect, is more important than applying a few rules so that you may look and feel better about yourself. That is the reason that Jesus was crucified on Calvary, meaning the Place of a Skull. (Mark 15:22)

Interestingly, as a type or shadow in my opinion, John the Baptist literally lost his head shortly after sending two of his followers to ask Jesus if He is the Messiah - intellect versus grace. It also depicts the message before and after the cross. John paved the way and addressed the heart through the intellect, but Jesus writes on the so-called tables of the heart with grace and love. Open up your heart to God so that His Spirit can write on it in the blood drenched language of the cross and Jesus Christ, the Word.

In Revelation 12:11 it says we will overcome by the blood of the Lamb and the word of our testimony. Is your testimony grounded on the Rock of Jesus and God's revealed Word in your Spirit? Eat and drink often of the living Bread and Wine. Partake in the communion with the Bread of the Word and the Wine of Life.

Then you will discover a deeper thirst for the sweeter wine – a thirst that can only be quenched by the Spirit. The Holy Spirit reveals the light, the life and the truth of the Living Word, Jesus Christ, in our hearts to transform our thoughts, our will and emotions, until Christ is formed in us and then we start thinking and doing like Him. When that happens, our fellowship with our Heavenly Father will become a cloud of manifested glory for a harvest that is ripe and a world that is hungry for the message of true hope and love, because His light will arise, and His glory will shine through us.

The only way of eating and consuming the Word, is by taking in the living Word, ie Jesus (Christological) Spirit quickened Word that explodes in your inner man. Everything else is only the letter - it kills as the letter kills, but the Spirit makes alive (2 Cor 3:6). It will also lead to religious and intellectual pride.

If the blood, the water and the Spirit does not testify with your spirit about Jesus, the lovely sweet savor of God will never ooze and pour out of your cells and being. On every cell the living Jesus are written, and thus every living cell in your body should call out "Jeshua!" (2 Cor 3, Rev 19:13) The fire of the Holy Spirit will then be upon you and will flow from you.

Then, and only then, we will experience the true fellowship of believers and the tangible presence (Shekinah glory) where angels join in the worship. This can only happen when at least 80% (100% is better) worship or call upon Jesus of one accord, or pray in their spiritual languages... because Jeshua is written on every cell in their bodies.

Then and only then, can one of heart, one body and one Spirit, one hope, one Lord, one faith, one baptism, one God and Father of all, who *is* above all and through all be manifested in His full awesome Shekinah glory in our midst (2 Cron 5:13, Acts 4:13, Heb 12:22). Then an innumerable company of angels can join us in worshipping, dancing, whirling and twirling and lying down in His total presence, light and life (Zeph 3:17).

Shout the Name of Jesus, cry the Name of Jesus and the weight of the Shekinah glory will soon press you to the floor...

May God bless each of you richly with wisdom, and revelation knowledge regarding His depths (Jer 33:3 and Rom 12:1-2), so that each of us can drink deeply from the depths and become part of His heart for us. Eat the roll of His book and let it melt like honey in your palate .... the part of heaven just above your tongue... when you speak let your words be as the words of God, or like apples of gold in a picture of silver. Let the sweet fragrance of Christ, a Holy Spirit anointing flowing through you, linger in the hearts and homes of other people.

Invitation

—ɯ—

If you haven't yet met Jesus, King of kings and Lord of lords ....call out to Him with everything in you from deep within, from your inner man, call upon....Jesus, Jesus, Jesus, Jesus until He explodes in your "inner Man".

Then sing the following song:

> *I've got the love of God in me*
> *I've got the love of God in me*
> *I've got His power,*
> *His might and His righteousness*
> *I've got the love of God in me*
>
> *Jesus Christ lives in my heart*
> *Jesus Christ lives in my heart*
> *Jesus Christ, the Son of God*
> *Jesus Christ live in my heart.*

- Get a Bible.
- Get baptised through immersion.
- Get Spirit baptised through laying on of hands by somebody that you can trust and who is really Spirit filled.
- Speak and often pray in your Spirit tongue.

- Go! Immediately go and start to win souls, make disciples and baptise them in the Name of Jesus, then immediately send them to do the same...

You don't need courses or seminaries or heavy teaching... you've got Jesus and the Holy Spirit and access to the Father immediately and fully. Over time He will reveal this given, factual, implanted gift to you. Go and conquer and win souls for Jesus. The most explosive growth in history in the Body of Christ is taking place in China. I believe in part because there is no church structure (buildings), no seminaries and no big named ministries and denominations - but raw childlike faith that the moment they are saved, they have the full power package of the indwelling Father, Son and Holy Spirit. What more do you want? Only believe.

Set the captives free, pray for the sick, do what Jesus tells you to do (see my book *So Who Are You Anyway?*)

I pray that the power of God, and God Himself will explode in you and work through you in order to touch others in a life changing way.

In the Name of Jesus Christ, King of all kings, I pray this for you and to everybody He sends to you as you journey through life.

Just a reminder of two prophetic insights:

The return of the King is near because undignified dancing like David, will destroy the religious demons and bring on the anointing in a powerful way. Release it, yes release it, sons and daughters, so that the King of glory may come in. Bring Him back through your nakedness and naked admiration and adoration of Father, Son and Holy Spirit.

Let the Scriptures speak to you, the oracles of God through the resurrection power of the Holy Spirit... resurrecting your inner self verse by verse ... Not dead letter upon dead letter and precept upon precept, but sword verse upon sword verse in the Holy Name of Jesus, son of the most High God... first-born amongst many who calls you His brother and My friend...He ain't heavy, He is my Brother... Spring up, oh well, from deep within me... Spirit-driven anointed sword Word of God.

Be Blessed, Be Bold, Be Free, Be Abundantly Prosperous in the Name of Jesus.

Please share your thoughts with us. We want to pray for you, answer your unanswered questions, and send you more materials.

Please visit the website of God With Us Ministries, www.godwithusmin.com for more Spirit-driven revelation and material.

Johan Fourie
God With Us Ministries

End Notes

—⟊—

1 Brother Yun with Paul Hattaway; *The Heavenly Man*, CSW, Monarch Books, p 245.

2 Brother Yun with Paul Hattaway; *The Heavenly Man*, CSW, Monarch Books, p 255.

3 Hendriks, Howard C and William, D; *Living By the Book*, Moody Press, 1991, p 10.

4 Foxe, John; *Foxe's Book of Martyrs*, Whitaker House, 1981.

5 Rutz, James; *Megashift*, Empowerment Press, 2005, p100.

6 Peterson, Eugene; *The Message, The Bible in Contemporary Language*, Navpress, 2004, p 8-9.

7 Murray, Andrew; *Andrew Murray on Prayer*, Whitaker House, 1998, p 14.

8 Wilkenson, Bruce, H; *The Vision of a Leader Study Guide*, World Teach, p 44.

[9] Henry, Matthew; *Concise Commentary on the Whole Bible*, OM Literature, 1995.

[10] Hendricks, Howard C and William, D; *Living By the Book*, Moody Press, 1991, p 9.

[11] Henry, Matthew; *Concise Commentary on the Whole Bible*, OM Literature, 1995.

[12] Henry, Matthew; *Concise Commentary on the Whole Bible*, OM Literature, 1995.

[13] Canfield, C, Hansen, M C, Spilchuck, B; *Chicken Soup for the Soul*, Health Communications, Inc, 1996, p 208.

[14] Hendricks, Howard C and William, D; *Living By the Book*, Moody Press, 1991, p 77.

[15] Easton, M G; *Illustrated Bible Dictionary*, Third Edition, Thomas Nelson, 1897.

[16] Varner, K; *Understanding Types, Shadows, and Names, A Biblical Guide Volume 1 & 2*, Destiny Image Publishers, Inc, 1996, 1997.

Notes: Hearing God's voice

—⁓—

God wants an intimate relationship with you, therefore He created you. He wants to communicate with you every single moment. He has no favourites and the ability to hear His voice and discern His counsel and direction, through His Word and the Holy Spirit, is available to you and to all His children. God has placed a yearning in your heart to be able to communicate with Him and He loves to communicate with you!

Sometimes people experience great difficulty in discerning the voice of our Heavenly Father, because they have the impression that it is a complicated or difficult thing. The truth is that it actually is a simple uncomplicated process – so uncomplicated that you should become like a child in order to grasp it.

As is the case with everything pertaining to our walk of faith, our Father never leaves us in the dark, for He is Light, and in Him there is no darkness. Therefore He provides the answer to hearing His voice in His Word:

I will stand on my watch and set myself on the tower, and will watch to see what He will say to me, and what I shall answer when I am reproved. And Jehovah answered me and said, Write the vision, and make it plain on the tablets, that he who reads it may run.
Hab 2:1-2

Habbakuk offers four keys to hearing God's voice:

1. Wait – Still yourself.
2. Keep watch and see – Fix your eyes upon Jesus.
3. Keep watch and listen.
4. Record it.

Wait

Quiet yourself. Ps 46:10 instruct us to be still:

"Be still and know that I am God."

Today, in our busy world, we have almost forgotten how to quiten ourselves and how to be still. It does not come naturally, although God intended it that way. Through the ages man has become used to being busy all the time, and therefore hearing God's voice will ask a personal choice and act of will from your side. God never stops communicating with us – however, we have lost the ability to hear and discern His voice in the busy, noisy world in which we live.

You and I have to make a conscious decision to take time out of our busy scedules and to retreat to a place where we can spend time at our Father's feet. Even Jesus, although He was in constant communion with the Father, took time out to spend alone on the mountain communing with God.

"And when He had sent the crowds away,
He went up into a mountain apart to pray.
And when evening had come, He was there alone."
Mat 14:23

Quiet yourself and get ready to receive. God is Spirit and where the Spirit is, there is liberty – i.e. freedom from your own limiting beliefs and human thought patterns. God communicates to your spirit through His Spirit:

*"These things we also speak, not in words which man's
wisdom teaches, but which the Holy Spirit teaches,
comparing spiritual things with spiritual. But the natural
man does not receive the things of the Spirit of God, for
they are foolishness to him;
neither can he know them, because they are spiritually
discerned."
1 Cor 2:13-14*

Therefore it is important to relax totally, to open up your spirit and to stop striving to hear. Ps 131:2 says the following:

*"Surely I have behaved and have quieted
my soul, as one weaned by its mother;
my soul on me is like one weaned..."*

That is how we should become quiet – totally relaxed and at ease as a baby just been weaned by its mother.

There are various ways to enter and to become quiet and responsive to receive from God:
- Listening to soaking music
- Softly praying in tongues
- Spirit led Bible reading.

Sometimes, the moment you decide to become quiet, the enemy will start bombarding you with everyday problems and tasks in order to hinder the communication process between you and God. A good way to deal with that is to keep a little notebook handy and to immediately write down all the things you should remember – the moment it is written down, you will relax, as you know you will not forget it.

Fix your eyes on Jesus
How did the prophets of old hear?

"And He said, hear now My words. If there is a prophet among you, I Jehovah will make Myself known to him in a vision, and will speak to him in a dream."
Numbers 12:6

As stated here in the Old Testament, God spoke to them through dreams and visions, which means that He communicated with them day and night. Jesus Christ is the same yesterday, today and forever (Heb 13:8). He is still communicating with us 24 hours a day.

He speaks primarily through images and pictures, as a picture paints a thousand words. More than 90 % of the Bible consists of pictures and images, while only 10 % is instruction. When God spoke to Abraham, he told him to look up to the sky and then prophesied that his descendants will outnumber the stars in the sky – much more powerful than only hearing it, was seeing it. God knows that He created man in such a manner that his memory has an amazing capacity to retain much more of an image seen than what is only heard. Therefore Jesus also taught through parables.

A vision is a spontaneous picture that appears spiritually. It can be in the form of a picture flashing through your mind's eye, or can appear during prayer, or even take the form of a trance where you are not conscious what is happening around you, as happened to Peter:

"And he became very hungry and desired to eat.
But while they made ready, an ecstasy fell on him.
And he saw the heaven opened and a certain vessel
like a sheet coming down to him, being bound at the
four corners and let down to the earth; in which were
all the four-footed animals of the earth, and the
wild beasts, and the reptiles, and the birds of the
heaven. And a voice came to him, saying, Rise, Peter!
Kill and eat!" Acts 10:10-13

In John 5:19 it is also stated that Jesus did what He saw His Father doing.

To fix your eyes on Jesus means to become quiet and to start focusing on Him and Him alone, not allowing any other thought to intrude. It also means that you become open and available to God's voice and visions, and that you have a child-like faith and expectation that He will communicate with you.

A number of blocks can prevent you from seeing:

- You may have a misconception that it is not a valid way of seeing and hearing God's voice.
- Your church culture or religion.
- You may be fearful – renounce all fear and believe 2 Tim 1:7:

> *"For God has not given us the spirit of fear, but of power and of love and of a sound mind."*

- If you experience sinful visions, repent and shut off all sinful visions in the name of Jesus Christ.
- You may have had bad experiences in the past which cause flashbacks. Take authority over such negative experiences and ask the Lord to protect you against it.

Keep watch and listen

How to recognize God's voice

Sometimes people are afraid that they will open themselves up to negative and evil forces when becoming quiet, because they do not know how to recognize God's voice. Again God teaches us in His Word how to recognize His voice:

*"And He said, Go forth and stand on the mountain before
Jehovah. And, behold, Jehovah passed by, and a great and
strong wind tore the mountains, and broke the rocks in
pieces before Jehovah.
But Jehovah was not in the wind.
And after the wind was an earthquake,
but Jehovah was not in the earthquake.
And after the earthquake was a fire,
but Jehovah was not in the fire.
And after the fire was a still, small voice.
1 Ki 19:11-12*

God's voice is a still, small voice, a gentle whisper – a
whisper that can be easily overrode by our own thoughts and
actions, if we are not attentive.

Pray beforehand that God will speak to you, and then
believe and receive it, thereby banishing all fearful thoughts
from your time spent with Him.

Your spirit will discern if you are hearing your own
thoughts, which usually are logical and analytical, thoughts
of the enemy that are evil, destructive and will unleash fear
and negative forces, or God's voice which will be creative,
gentle, kind and loving and will bring you life, peace, love
and comfort, as the Holy Spirit is your Comforter.

In 2 Cor 10:4-5 we read the following:

*"For the weapons of our warfare are not fleshly, but mighty
through God to the pulling down of strongholds, pulling
down imaginations and every high thing (thought) that
exalts itself against the knowledge of God,
and bringing into captivity every thought into
the obedience of Christ;"*

You will immediately discern evil or even your own
thoughts that is contradictory to the Word of God and to the

leading of the Holy Spirit. Therefore, there need not be any fear when entering a place of quietness and communion with God – He will meet you there and come and minister to you His love, kindness, peace, joy and wisdom!

The Hebrew word for prophesy is "naba" which means to bubble up. God's voice will usually occur as a spontaneous interruption, literally bubbling up. You may be busy reading the Bible, and from nowhere a spontaneous thought or vision literally drops or bubbles up in your mind/spirit. The Holy Spirit will release a river of thoughts in you, if you allow Him. God's voice will almost always be in the first person, because He communicates with you on an intimate and personal level. He desires a close relationship with you, therefore there will not be distance and formality – He will speak to you as a loving Father speaks to the son or daughter He adores.

Record it
In Revelation 1:11 the Lord instructs John:

"…Also, What you see, write in a book…"

Therefore you should also write down what the Lord told you. The moment it is recorded in ink, the enemy cannot come and lie to you or throw forgetfulness at you – it will become a precious possession, which will strengthen your faith in times of need, and a legacy to your children and grandchildren.

Another important reason to record it is that it is a manifestation of the Holy Spirit and controlled by the Holy Spirit. It can be in the form of questions that you asked the Lord, words you heard, or visions or pictures you saw. Always record in the 1st person – God is a God of intimate and loving relationships and will not be distant or impersonal – His voice will be edifying and loving.

You are a unique human being – God created you that way. He knows you, your likes, dislikes, feelings, circumstances, and even the way you like to hear, intimately for He created you – He will honour that because He knows that is the way you will be able to communicate with Him. Do not compare yourself with others – look only to your Heavenly Father who loves and adores you!

A word of caution – a human tendency is to immediately start to analyze and explain everything we hear – even our Father's voice! Do not fall into that trap - faith is not natural, logical and analytical, but creative, unexplainable, and spiritual!

If you experience any doubt concerning the message you heard from God, ask Him for confirmation. He is the Creator of the universe and will use His Word, people, books and other creative ways to confirm His message. He is a gracious, loving Father and will not let you live in uncertainty – He promises in His word:

Call to Me, and I will answer you, and show you great and inscrutable things which you do not know.
Jer 33:3

Marié Fourie

Other books by Johan Fourie

Coming soon:

So Who Are You Anyway?

There Is Gold On Your Inside!

Streams of Honey

You may contact the author at:

Johan Fourie
P O Box 765
Robertson
6705
South Africa

or

E-mail: johanfourie@godwithusmin.com

or

Visit our website:

www.godwithusmin.com

Printed in the United States
79552LV00002B/51

9 781602 662964